The SUPERVISOR'S *Desktop Library*

GENE GAROFALO

PRENTICE HALL
Career and Personal Development
Englewood Cliffs, NJ 07632

Simon & Schuster, A Paramount Communications Company

Prentice-Hall International (UK) Limited, *London*
Prentice-Hall of Australia Pty. Limited, *Sydney*
Prentice-Hall Canada, Inc., *Toronto*
Prentice-Hall Hispanoamericana, S.A., *Mexico*
Prentice-Hall of India Private Limited, *New Delhi*
Prentice-Hall of Japan, Inc., *Tokyo*
Simon & Schuster Asia Pte. Ltd., *Singapore*
Editora Prentice-Hall do Brasil, Ltda., *Rio de Janeiro*

©1995 *by*
PRENTICE HALL, Inc.
Englewood Cliffs, NJ

10 9 8 7 6 5 4 3 2 1

ISBN 0-13-146986-X

9 780131 469860   90000

PRENTICE HALL
Career and Personal Development
Englewood Cliffs, NJ 07632
Simon & Schuster, A Paramount Communications Company

Printed in the United States of America

C O N T E N T S

ix

Introduction

This book is about, in fact every book in this series is about, learning how to do a better job as a supervisor. We start with communicating because it is the single most important skill a supervisor must master. No two supervisors jobs are exactly alike, but every supervisor must learn how to communicate. It is a basic requirement for anyone who hopes to direct the activities of others.

Communication literally means *sharing*. In business it applies to the transfer of information, instructions, knowledge, news, opinions, and so forth from one person to another, or others. It is an interchange of thoughts or interests, *the act of giving and receiving*.

Why is this skill so important to supervisors? Because in most organizations they are the company's communication hubs. They receive directions from senior management and pass them along to line employees.

This handbook describes the communication process. We begin with how to listen, which is the first step in effective communication. Any supervisor who believes that communication begins and ends with passing out orders to employees is badly mistaken—and in dire need of the material contained in these pages.

This book will detail the various methods of communication from verbal, to written, to tone of voice. We'll suggest the right method to fit various situations. We'll tell you how to give precise verbal and written instructions, how to ask questions, how to better understand others, how to write memos that get action, how to write proposals that will get you noticed by senior management, and how to help the people who report to you become better communicators. There's a chapter on training because all training requires excellent communication skills.

The reward for becoming a better communicator comes through improved performance. The department's results will improve. Things will get done on time. There will be fewer surprises, fewer brush fires to put out. Relationships with other departments will be good. Employee morale will be high because staff members will know what is expected, and most important, they will have a supervisor who listens. Senior members of management will be impressed because they'll have a department manager who understands directions and is able to carry them out. (When members of management talk about "key employees," they mean those who are good communicators.)

The investment needed to acquire these rewards is the time it takes to read the material carefully. It is an investment that will pay dividends for years to come.

1

Why Mastering Communication Skills is Important

Leadership and communication are inseparable.
You can't have one without the other.
— Claude I. Taylor,
Chairman of the Board, Air Canada

The Supervisor's Function
as a Link Between
Senior Management and Line Employees

In any organization the supervisor's role is to carry out the directions of senior management. Supervisors are like line officers in an army. They take instructions and orders from the high brass and translate them for the troops. They are the action people who make things happen. It is their responsibility to understand everything that needs to be done and then to act to get those things done. Their contribution is vital to the success of any business operation.

The key to making this contribution is communication, which simply means understanding others and being understood in turn. It is a big part of a supervisor's job. Most of a supervisor's day is spent in some sort of communication with others both in and outside the organization. These "verbal transactions," or communications, take place in a variety of ways, for example,

In formal meetings
In informal contacts
By telephone
By facsimile machine
By computer (electronic mail)
By memo
By formal report

All these methods involve a transfer of information. They all require rock-solid communication skills.

THE DIFFERENT COMMUNICATION LEVELS

The first step toward effective communication is understanding others. That means learning how to listen. Not many people think of listening as a skill, but it is, and it's one of the most important skills any supervisor can acquire. We'll discuss the steps toward becoming an effective listener in Chapter Two. For now, let's concentrate on the different levels of communication required by the supervisor.

In most business organizations supervisors will be in contact with

1. Senior and middle managers.
2. Employees who report to the supervisor (staff members).

3. Peers (other supervisors).
4. Employees who report to other supervisors.
5. Customers (usually those customers with a request, grievance, or problem).
6. Suppliers of products or services.
7. Information seekers such as prospects, stockbrokers, job seekers, auditors, consultants, and so forth.

Each one of these groups is relying on the supervisor to provide a different level of communication, a different level of information and understanding. Each group wants something different from the supervisor. Let's examine the expectations of each group.

COMMUNICATING WITH MANAGEMENT

What management expects from supervisors is the ability to take instructions to translate them for line employees and see that the instructions are carried out. In fact, carrying out the directions of management is the supervisor's most important role.

Before an instruction, or direction, can be carried out it must be understood. Let's see what directions are all about.

Essentially, any direction from management can be broken down into three basic parts:

1. What needs to get done
2. How it will get done
3. When it needs to get done (the priority of the task)

In discussions with management, make sure that these three elements of a direction are clear. If any element is hazy, ask questions until the "clouds" have dissipated. Most often, the "what" and "when" of a task are dictated. The supervisor will frequently be allowed input as to "how."

How Communication
with Management Works

For the supervisor, communication with management is both downward and upward. The downward part occurs when managers near the top of the organization send instructions and requirements via the supervisor to line employees. The supervisor is more than a mere transfer agent. He or she has the responsibility to implement the directions.

Directions sometimes come in the form of requests, but seasoned supervisors recognize them as orders that must be followed. It is usually most uncomfortable when a supervisor has incorrectly translated what management requires. That is why it's important to clarify the three elements of a direction: what, how, and when.

If instructions flow downward, information heads upstream. Supervisors are required to report back to management on how much success they have had carrying out instructions. These progress reports may be formal or informal, verbal or in writing, but supervisors should recognize that they will be judged by their contents.

In any progress report management wants the following information in one form or another:

1. Are we on schedule?
2. If not, what needs to be done to get back on schedule?
3. What future problems are foreseen that could knock us off schedule?

Career Hint: *If you want to acquire a reputation as a supervisor who is on top of the job, you must know where you are on all projects, know where you are going, and know how you're going to get there.* That's the kind of information that management wants communicated. The supervisor who frustrates management is the one who doesn't quite seem to have a handle on what's going on.

ONE-ON-ONE MEETINGS WITH SENIOR MANAGERS

Many meetings with management are on an informal, one-on-one basis. They take place in hallways, outside lunchrooms, or in private offices. Often, instructions critical to an operation are communicated during these informal sessions. Supervisors should be careful to clarify any such instructions. If they differ substantially from previously received instructions, it may be a good idea to confirm them in writing.

HOW TO GET THE MOST OUT OF GROUP MEETINGS WITH SENIOR MANAGEMENT

Management has just called a meeting. You don't know what it is about, but something tells you it's important. What's the best way to prepare for such a meeting? Supervisors who follow these suggestions will get the most out of such sessions:

1. Ask about the meeting's subject matter in advance. If possible, get a written agenda. Knowing what will be discussed will help you be prepared and in a position to make a contribution.
2. Arrive on time. Tardiness communicates rudeness. It's a poor way to begin a meeting.
3. Note the names and titles of the attendees. It's often a good idea to write down the attendance list on a

note pad. Who is present can tell you much about the priority management attaches to the subject matter.

4. Note the format of the meeting. If there are one or two speakers behind a lectern and holding a microphone hostage, there's a good chance that whatever is being discussed has already been decided. You're going to get directions on carved, stone tablets. On the other hand, if the format is a free-for-all round table discussion, chances are final decisions have yet to be made.

5. Listen attentively. Make sure there is clear understanding of all the points covered.

6. Ask questions. Don't be afraid of appearing ignorant or stupid. If you don't understand the material, it's the fault of the person making the presentation, not yours. Make sure, however, that any questions you ask are relevant to the subject matter.

7. Be open to the subject matter. A closed or negative attitude is quickly sensed.

8. Take notes. Written notations are invaluable after the meeting is over and memory fades. If someone else is taking the minutes of the meeting, make sure you're on the list to receive a copy.

9. On those items that affect your area, summarize your understanding of what was discussed and what your responsibilities become after the meeting is over. This procedure is particularly important when given directions.

10. State opinions and objections clearly. If there's a ghost in the machine, make its presence known. Do not, however, keep repeating the same objection over and over. Your boss heard you the first time. Mention obstacles and problems that stand in the

way of getting the job done. Also discuss solutions to these problems. (As a general rule, never bring up a problem without also offering a solution.)

11. Feel free to offer alternatives if you believe they represent a better way to get the job done.

12. When speaking to the group, be short, be clear, and be to the point. Have facts available to support any statements.

13. Summarize the meeting to yourself when it is completed. Have a clear idea of what senior management expects to happen next.

14. Follow up and keep all promises.

15. *Never* make comments or discuss problems with individuals; rather, address the group at large.

16. Don't worry about the other person's turf. If you foresee a problem in another area that doesn't affect your operation, ignore it.

The following is a worksheet that can be helpful in supervisor–management meetings.

Meeting Worksheet

Meeting Worksheet

Date_____

Attendees _____

_____

_____

Subjects Discussed_____

_____

_____

_____

Conclusions Reached_____

_____

_____

New Instructions

1. _____

_____

_____

Results Expected _____

_____

By When _____

Reports Required _____

_____

2. _____

_____

_____

Results Expected _____

_____

By When _____

Reports Required _____

_____

3. _____

_____

_____

Results Expected _____

_____

By When _____

Reports Required _____

_____

FIVE RULES WHEN
COMMUNICATING WITH MANAGEMENT

The first rule of communication with management is *to understand what management wants done.* You can't translate directions to line employees if you don't understand them yourself. If there are any questions or if the directions are unclear, ask questions or request clarification before proceeding. Thoughtful questions not only lead to better understanding of what needs to be done, they often result in changes to the original instructions because the senior manager is required to think through the implications of what has been requested. A few minutes spent in nailing down the direction may save days (or a reputation) later on.

The second rule is to *make sure the direction is specific.* Don't meekly accept very general directions that may be interpreted several different ways. If the direction is general, the results, from management's view, will never be satisfactory.

The third rule is that it is all right to disagree, but within limits. *It is usually acceptable for supervisors to disagree with senior management over the method for getting something done, but not over the objective itself.* Supervisors are those who implement policy. They have every right to discuss the details of how that policy will get accomplished. They are not, however, policy makers, and any attempt to intrude into this area will be viewed negatively.

The fourth rule is to *obtain agreement on the resources that will be available to do the job required.* A supervisor may be told that some task has a high priority and then later be reprimanded for authorizing overtime to get that task accomplished. (The amount of resources that management is willing to allot to a task is a better gauge of that tasks' priority than any lip service about its importance.)

The fifth rule is to *determine how often and in what form management wants the results reported*. Remember, earlier, we stated that business communication flowed both downward and upward? Reporting the results of various programs and activities to senior management is an important supervisory task. It is an example of communicating upward.

Every one of these rules for communicating with management is aimed at the same objectives: They are to understand what management wants accomplished and to report back on the success of getting those things accomplished.

COMMUNICATING WITH MANAGEMENT SUMMARY

In summary, when faced with a management direction ask the following questions:

1. What does management want done?
2. What are the specific objectives of this task?
3. What is the best way to get this task accomplished?
4. What resources is the company prepared to commit to the project?
5. How does the reporting work? What gets reported? When does it get reported? To whom does it get reported? In what format is the information required?

COMMUNICATING WITH STAFF MEMBERS: AN ELEVEN-STEP PROCESS DESIGNED TO TRANSLATE MANAGEMENT OBJECTIVES TO LINE EMPLOYEES

There is a critical time after the supervisor receives directions from management. It is the time when the supervisor translates these directions for line employees and makes sure they are understood and implemented. Changes have to be "sold." In addition to communicating new requirements, supervisors must learn how to be persuasive.

Here's an eleven-step communication process for getting line employees to understand the requirements for a new company program:

1. Know what you want to say about the program. Prepare instructions in advance. Set up all conditions of the staff meeting, including the meeting room, the presentation aids, the support needed from others, and so forth.

2. Be positive about the project. (Don't apologize to the staff because management has come up with another "damn fool" idea.) When discussing implementation plans, use "we" instead of "I" and "you." Emphasize that the program is a team effort.

3. To support the team concept further, consult with key employees beforehand. Let them handle segments of the presentation. This not only demonstrates thoughtful preparation, it indicates that other employees are behind the project.

4. Give all instructions on a step-by-step basis. Keep the steps simple and easy to understand. Compartmentalize the work.

5. Ask for contributions from employees on how goals can be met. Use a system that encourages these contributions, such as writing them down on a blackboard for all to see.

6. Don't cut off negative comments, but hear them through. Show that you listen. Ask for suggestions on how problems can be overcome.

7. Don't hide information. Be open.

8. Don't be afraid to acknowledge an obstacle that hadn't

been considered before an employee brought it up in open session. However, leave the impression that no obstacle is insurmountable.

9. Set timetables and give assignments. Make sure that you are responsible for several of the dirty job assignments that no one else wants.

10. Set up a reporting structure. Remember that senior management expects supervisors to know where they are.

11. Keep the door open. Ideas may occur to staff members long after the meeting is over.

BUILDING AN INTRADEPARTMENTAL COMMUNICATION SYSTEM

At one time or another every supervisor has been handed a surprise by a staff member. A requested report is turned in incomplete or in a format other than that requested, a vital project is delayed with no advance warning, a problem is swept under the rug where it grows into a monster. These situations are embarrassing because it appears to senior management as if the supervisor doesn't know what's going on in his or her own backyard.

Unwanted surprises are caused by, to quote the warden in *Cool Hand Luke*, "a failure to communicate." The failure is the responsibility of the supervisor. If staff members aren't reporting important data, it's because the supervisor hasn't established the proper reporting system.

The first thing every supervisor should do upon appointment to the position is establish a reporting system that will monitor everything important that's going on within the department. The operative word is *important,* because the supervisor can't afford to become bogged down in details.

Here's how such an information system can be established:

1. Set the right example by communicating important information to staff members. Tell your staff members why certain projects are important. Conduct regularly scheduled meetings during which information is exchanged. Be open and forthright. Staff members will be open and forthright in return.

2. Make sure instructions are understood. Ask for feedback from staff members on their interpretation of assignments. Follow up verbal instructions in writing.

3. Insist that staff members participate. People are more alert when they know they're expected to contribute.

4. When giving assignments, establish a series of progress reports to be supplied by staff members that will help determine if a project is on schedule.

5. Don't reprimand staff members who bring bad news or confess mistakes. If you do next time, they'll conceal this information as long as possible.

6. Set up standards of performance and measure actual performance against these standards. If the department should be cranking out 120 orders a day and suddenly output slows to 50 orders per day, the numbers themselves have "communicated" the existence of a problem.

7. Occasionally ask to see actual samples of work in progress. Praise what's good. Correct what's wrong without reprimand, unless, of course, the correction

has been given before without effect.

8. Be accessible. An open office door is a tacit invitation to come inside and discuss problems.

9. Let your staff members know why information must be complete. Offer guidance, encouragement, and coaching. ("This is a good beginning, Eddie, but we still need an estimate of the total worker-hours allocated to complete this project.")

10. Let your staff members know that you don't like surprises. Remind them of Henry Kissinger's advice: "What must be revealed eventually should be revealed immediately."

11. Be genuinely interested in your staff members and what they have to say. People like to talk to those who are interested in them.

12. Be sparing with criticism and free with praise. The employee who is criticized won't "open up" next time. The employee who is praised will be anxious to come back with more information.

If you do all these things, you'll be the best informed supervisor in the company. Everyone will envy your communication system and your rapport with employees.

COMMUNICATING WITH EMPLOYEES WHO REPORT TO OTHER SUPERVISORS

To complete assignments, cooperation from employees in other departments is often necessary. This situation can create problems. A direction given to an employee who reports to someone else may be regarded as an intrusion on another's "turf." Supervisors should consider their own reaction when another person attempts to give directions to their staff members.

That's why communication with employees from other departments should primarily be conducted through that other department's supervisor. It's a simple courtesy that most supervisors will reciprocate. That doesn't mean the supervisor can't contact an employee for different kinds of information. Informal communication is inevitable.

Here are a few simple rules when communicating with employees of other departments:

1. Any requests that will take up the employee's time should be made through the employee's supervisor.
2. Any complaints about the employee's performance should be made to the supervisor.
3. When an employee in another department will be spending time on a project that affects yours, it's okay to provide instructions and details on what is wanted. Be sure, however, that the employee's supervisor is informed.
4. Show appreciation by praising good work.

THE SUPERVISOR'S ROLE IN COMMUNICATING TO CUSTOMERS

In many different industries supervisors come in contact with company customers either in person or by phone. In other instances supervisors are required to correspond with customers. In most of these circumstances the contact concerns

A customer request for service

An inquiry about the product

A complaint about the product or service

A problem that must be resolved

Communication skills are extremely important in these instances because the customer is either unhappy with the company's performance or wants something done. The supervisor represents company management to the customer, someone who can resolve an unhappy situation or unsnarl red tape. The customer's problem must be understood and action taken to resolve that problem. Tact and diplomacy are vital.

When speaking with customers, remember the rules for communicating with senior management. Customers are, after all, the most senior management in charge of any company. When they take their business away, the company ceases to exist. Consider their requests as directions. Break down the directions into elements (what, how, when).

EIGHT COMMUNICATION RULES WHEN DEALING WITH UNHAPPY CUSTOMERS

1. Listen closely to learn what the customer wants done. Patience is almost always required. If the customer is unhappy, he or she may wish to spend a few minutes reciting the company's sins. Patient listening often deflects frustration and anger.

2. Get to the root of the problem. Repeat the problem as you understand it. Get agreement from the customer that the problem is as stated. This alone will often reduce tension because the customer is relieved to be, at last, understood.

3. Whenever possible, avoid like the plague the "it's not my job" type of response. If the problem falls outside your particular area of responsibility, offer to connect the customer to the right department and make sure someone is fielding the call.

4. Determine what action would resolve the problem. Is this action within your jurisdiction? If so, offer the customer the solution. Make sure the customer understands what will be done and the timetable needed to do it. Don't make promises that can't be kept or commitments that are beyond your level of authority.

5. If the problem's correction requires a higher level of authority, make the communication necessary to obtain it.

6. Make written notes to ensure that promises made will be remembered and acted upon. (The purpose of the written note is to communicate with yourself. This is, and always has been, an important communication highway.)

7. Follow through after the fact to make sure the customer is satisfied with the result. What is being communicated now to the customer is concern over his or her opinion of the company and its service.

8. If the same problems and complaints keep recurring with many different customers, communicate this fact to senior management. The company is doing something wrong, and it needs to be corrected.

COMMUNICATING WITH PEERS: THE KEY TO GETTING THINGS DONE

The larger the organization the more important it is for supervisors to obtain the cooperation of their fellow supervisors in other departments. Supervisors are the action people who get things done. They can help, or hinder, their peers. No supervisor, no department, exists in a vacuum.

Tasks and responsibilities are interrelated.

The supervisors with "tunnel vision," those whose line of sight is limited to what is directly before them, who think only of their own priorities, often wonder why they can't get their peers to work with them.

Cooperation between supervisors means much more than "You wash my back, I'll wash yours." It requires a clear understanding and respect for the other person's objectives. It requires an understanding of corporate objectives as well. In short, it requires *communication*.

CONNECTING WITH OTHER SUPERVISORS ON A ONE-ON-ONE BASIS

The most common communication between supervisors takes place informally, face to face. Much of the company's internal business is conducted in this manner. As with all forms of communication, the goal is to "connect," that is, to understand and be understood.

For the supervisor who wishes to connect with peers on a one-on-one basis, here's how to go about it:

1. Learn all about the objectives and priorities of the other supervisor. Learn how his or her department operates and the functions it performs for the company.

2. Learn how the operation of your peer's department affects your department. What work does it perform that is vital to your department?

3. Learn what the other department expects from your department. Is this expectation reasonable?

4. Learn what you can do to help the other person's operation. For example, your department might be turning over edited and credit-approved orders to the warehouse for order picking at 3:00 P.M. every afternoon. Perhaps the freight forwarder shows up at 2:00 P.M., and many orders could be shipped a full day earlier if the paperwork arrived by noon. A slight change in your department's operation to send some orders down by noon could make the warehouse supervisor's performance look a lot better.

5. If any other supervisor offers a complaint about your operation, don't be defensive; rather, listen with the thought of making corrections.

6. Assume that other supervisors always have the good of the company in mind, just as you do.

7. Make a conscious effort to establish relationships. Have coffee or lunch with other supervisors so you can have discussions on an informal basis.

   Get to know others in the Dept.

8. Root for other supervisors to succeed and do well. Your positive attitude will show up in your relations with them.

9. Never complain about the actions, or lack of action, of another supervisor to senior management without first discussing it with that person.

10. Always try to correct any problems or differences of opinion between the two of you without appealing to senior management.

In summary, the key to cooperation among peers is through understanding the other person's point of view. The first step toward understanding others is effective communication.

SUPERVISOR COUNCILS

Companies can assist supervisors' mutual communication through regularly scheduled meetings in which common problems are discussed. A clear agenda will result in a more productive meeting, but time should also be available for free-form discussions in which any subject may be raised. These meetings often work best when there is no member of senior management present. Discussions are frequently more frank when the brass is absent. The moderator can be a middle manager, or another supervisor.

If such a "supervisors' council" does not exist at your company, suggest that one be formed. If there is enough support from other supervisors, there's no reason why such a request should be refused. These councils should be run by and for the benefit of supervisors. Of course, it's important that the meetings not turn into gripe sessions, but rather be called to address legitimate operational issues.

The meetings can be expanded in several different ways. Guest speakers can be brought in from both inside and outside the company to provide information on a variety of subjects. Recommendations can be made to senior management. These councils can have a positive benefit both to the company and the supervisors who take part.

Learn about and tap into networks

COMMUNICATING WITH SUPPLIERS

Supervisors often are in contact with the representatives of organizations who provide goods and services to the company. That's because supervisors may be responsible for the actual use of these goods and services even though the purchasing decisions are made by others. The critical factor in these kinds of communications is for the supervisor not to make commitments that bind the company, or to provide information that may be considered confidential. Good rules to follow are

1. Learn and follow the company regulations regarding contacts with suppliers.
2. Document any problems with suppliers' products. Do allow suppliers the opportunity to correct small problems before they become a "big deal."
3. Don't play favorites because of personal relationships with some supplier representatives.
4. Never provide endorsements unless specifically permitted to do so by company management.

COMMUNICATING WITH INFORMATION SEEKERS

Supervisors are a source for information and that means they will be sought out be people outside the company, such as auditors, consultants hired by the company for a specific purpose, and so forth, who want this information. In these instances, it is prudent to observe a few simple rules:

1. Make sure that you are authorized to provide the information. When in doubt, get the authorization in writing.
2. Assign someone to work with the information seeker.
3. Provide only the data that is requested. In fact, take a narrow interpretation of the request. Don't volunteer.
4. Provide management with a copy of all information given to outsiders.
5. Don't give anyone, auditors and government tax examiners excepted, blanket access to company files.
6. Inform staff members of the project if a "stranger" will be on the premises. This will help dispel any rumors.

FOUR FLOW CHARTS THAT SHOW
THE TYPICAL LINES OF
COMMUNICATION IN LARGE CORPORATIONS

Downward-Upward Communication

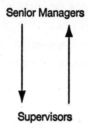

Trickle-Down Communication

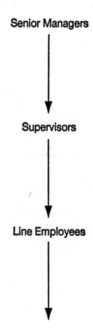

Lateral Communication

Supervisors ←——————→ Other Supervisors

Diagonal Communication

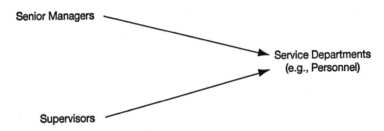

Senior Managers

Service Departments
(e.g., Personnel)

Supervisors

HOW TO MAKE SURE YOU'RE PLUGGED INTO THE COMPANY'S COMMUNICATION AND INFORMATION NETWORK

Are you always the last to know what's going on in the company, even for those things that directly affect your department? Are changes put into place without consulting you? Perhaps you're not properly plugged into the company's communication network. Just because you have an office and a nameplate on the desk doesn't automatically get you hooked into the system. Being left in the cold can be dangerous, because you sometimes won't have enough time to assess and react to a situation. It also can be personally demoralizing, as if your opinion didn't matter. If you are being left out, here's how to worm your way in:

1. Don't take the omission personally. Not being included in important memos may be an oversight, rather than a deliberate snub. Also, don't assume

you have a right to know everything that goes on. If it doesn't affect your department, it doesn't matter.

2. Read thoroughly every piece of paper that does come across your desk. Perhaps some of the information you suspect has been deliberately kept from you is included in that dull, six-page memo you threw away without finishing.

3. Faithfully attend every scheduled meeting. Meeting attendees are usually copied on memos of the actions that result from these sessions. Attending meetings is a way to demonstrate that you're interested in what's going on.

4. If not included on a memo that directly affects your operation, call the sender and *gently* ask the reason for the omission. You'll usually get a belated copy, and the oversight is not likely to happen again.

5. Be sure that all interested parties are copied on the memos you write. It's the best way to make sure the favor will be returned.

6. After receipt of a thoughtful memo, call the sender and thank her. Most memo writers are so anxious for readers, you'll surely be on the list from now on.

7. Memos aren't the only way information gets transferred. Most information is communicated verbally, often on a "by the way" basis. Establish a network of friends and acquaintances in the company whom you trust. Spend time with them. Attend company functions.

8. Never betray confidences. One of the ways to obtain information is by being known as someone who can be trusted with it.

9. Offer your confidence to those you know you can trust. People will be flattered—and reciprocate.

10. Never appear to pry or snoop. There's a tendency to

withhold information from those who appear to be anxious to possess it.

11. If your company uses computers, start to communicate with others via electronic mail, bulletin boards, and so forth.

SUMMARY

The supervisor has two basic roles. The first is to take directions from senior management and pass them along to line employees. The second is to inform management of the results of their instructions. These functions are key to the success of any business organization.

To fulfill their roles, supervisors must become good communicators. They must be able to understand what management wants done and be able to communicate these requirements to staff members.

The first step in becoming a good communicator is by learning how to listen. Listening is more than just paying attention to words. A good listener tries to understand the message the speaker wishes to convey.

In most business organizations supervisors come in contact with many individuals both inside and outside the company. Their communication skills must be diverse to interact with the many people they meet.

Communication with management is top down. Management gives instructions. Supervisors report back on the results of carrying out these instructions.

It's important for supervisors to be well prepared for

meetings with management in which directions and instructions are discussed.

It is the supervisor's job to translate management objectives to line employees and to see that these objectives are met.

The first thing every supervisor should do upon being appointed to the position is to establish a reporting system that provides information on everything important going on within the department.

To gain the cooperation of their peers, supervisors must learn how to communicate with other department heads and supervisors within the organization. This means learning what peers want and helping them achieve it.

Supervisors must be careful not to exert "authority" when communicating with company employees who report to others within the organization.

Communicating with customers is similar to communicating with management. Learn what the customer wants and then try to provide it.

When communicating with suppliers and people outside the company who seek information, supervisors must follow company guidelines.

2

The Communication Process

*Precision in communication is more
important than ever.*
— James Thurber

THE SEVEN HABITS
OF ALL EFFECTIVE COMMUNICATORS

Outside of perhaps rehearsing for a speech or rewriting memos, no one "practices" communication. For most supervisors, this necessary skill must be learned on the job. Every encounter with another employee can be considered a learning experience. In these encounters supervisors learn the importance of communicating precise meanings. Even a small difference between what is meant and what is understood can lead to disaster.

Observing the habits of those who seem to have a natural talent for getting their messages delivered and understood is a good way to learn how to communicate with precision. Most of us have met someone who has the label of being a "great communicator." What, exactly, do these communicators do that make them "great"?

They may employ vastly different styles of delivery, but good communicators share several things in common. Here are the habits good communicators employ to make sure their message is getting across:

1. Good communicators learn how to listen. They don't just listen to be polite. They have a keen interest in what the other person has to say. *They want the other person's message.*

2. Good communicators put their own thoughts in order before trying them out on others. Their presentations are organized. Ideas seem to flow naturally from them, one point to the next in a logical sequence.

3. Good communicators speak and write simply. They recognize that the purpose of communication is not to impress the listener or reader with their own knowledge, but to transfer information. *The message to be delivered takes precedence over their egos.*

4. Good communicators don't overwhelm the audience with too much information. They realize, sadly perhaps, that only so much information delivered in a single presentation will be retained. They select several important points they want remembered, and they emphasize these points several different ways. *Repetition is an important factor in communication.*

5. Good communicators "set the stage" for their remarks. They engage several of the audience's five senses (touch, smell, sight, sound, taste) through the use of visual displays, props, sound, and so forth.

6. Good communicators appeal to emotion and the audience's self-interest. Both the evangelist preaching eternal salvation and the financial analyst suggesting a once-in-a-lifetime investment opportunity are offering their listeners a "profit."

7. Good communicators truly believe what they are saying. The insincere, the liars, are recognized
   sooner or later.

Is it easy to acquire these habits? Of course not! They require a
conscious effort and much practice. But they can be learned.
Take baby steps. Start with sincerity when speaking and a
determination to really listen when others speak. Move on to
organizing your thoughts. Never stop practicing improving your
communication skills.

SELECTING THE RIGHT METHOD OF COMMUNICATION TO FIT THE SITUATION

Communication can be conducted in a variety of ways from an
off-the-cuff comment made when passing an employee in the
hall to a formal letter to a peer with copies to everyone in the
company fortunate to occupy a desk. Different approaches fit
different situations. Suggestions are usually best delivered verbally. A change in procedure almost always requires written
documentation.

Often, the method of delivery "communicates" as much as
the actual content. ("The medium is the message.") Written
communications carry more weight because they are an unde-
niable and recoverable record. There's something about the
printed page that makes it seem more "official." A direction,
when given verbally, may appear to be "no big deal."

The following are suggestions for communication methods to fit common business situations:

DIRECTIONS TO STAFF MEMBERS

Most orders to employees are given verbally. It is not practical to put every direction in writing. When phrased as suggestions or requests, orders appear less "official," but they still
carry the weight of a command. When giving a direction,

what should always be communicated by the supervisor is the expectation that the direction will be carried out.

NEW POLICIES AND PROCEDURES

Any new policy or procedure required of employees should always be put in writing. The procedures should be fully detailed so each employee knows exactly what is required. Meetings to discuss the procedures are also a good idea.

When instituting a new procedure, a feedback system should be set up to determine if the procedure is being carried out and its impact on the operation. It's up to the supervisor to set up this system and to appoint personnel responsible for the reporting.

WARNINGS FOR SLOPPY WORK OR INAPPROPRIATE BEHAVIOR

The kind of warning given to an employee is dependent on the offense. For a slight or first-time offense, an informal, verbal warning may be best because it won't appear in the employee's file. Warnings for more serious work infractions or for repeated offenses, or for any matter that could lead to dismissal, must be given in writing. With so many employees suing companies over wrongful dismissal, it's important to establish a paper "trail" showing why the employee was let go.

Before giving any warning for sloppy work, the supervisor must make sure that the employee was properly trained. Additional training is often a better solution than discipline.

REPORTS TO SENIOR MANAGEMENT

Supervisors usually have no choice as to the method of communication with senior management. Management tells the supervisor what is required. Written reports are usually required. These should be carefully and thoughtfully prepared. Supervisors should discuss the reporting methods with the managers who require them. They should also follow up after the reports have been delivered to make sure the format and content are satisfactory.

Career Hint: *When reporting to senior management, anticipate any additional information not contained in the report that may be requested and have that information available.* This practice will give the supervisor the reputation of someone who is on top of the job.

REQUESTS OF OTHER DEPARTMENTS

The communication method used with peers in other departments depends on the weight of the request. Make most requests casual, such as; "Joe, could you possibly deliver the processed orders up to our department before noon? That way we'll be able to get the bulk of the work out the door the same day." This kind of request may be more effective than a formal memo, which the other supervisor may consider a challenge.

Career Hint: *Always provide an explanation for a request when communicating with other department heads.* It is a courtesy that will be appreciated.

In instances when verbal requests have been ignored, a written memo with copies to the proper level of management may be appropriate.

PROBLEMS

The truth about problems is that no one wants to hear about them. That means the fewer problems communicated to senior management, the better. Before relaying any problem to senior management, *first try to fix it.* Management treasures supervisors who are able to handle most situations without intervention from above.

When it is necessary to communicate a problem, also offer a solution. Be sure to detail the problem in writing, but give just as much effort to the proposed solution. When writing about problems, don't be a Calamity Jane by predicting dire consequences if things aren't fixed.

Fact of Corporate Life: *Many of the problems communicated to management will be ignored. Expect this reaction and experience less frustration. Do not, however, let this deter you from reporting the problems.*

In summary, the method of communication chosen in a situation is largely a matter of common sense. Verbal communications are not as "official" as those that are written.

How to Listen, the First Step in Effective Communication

Everyone knows how to listen, right? It's an inborn ability, like eating and drinking. Then why don't we get more out of what other people tell us? Why do we often walk away from conversations with only a dim idea of what the other person's message was? It is because most of us don't regard listening as a skill that must be acquired and cultivated like any other. Learning to listen is not a priority for most folks, but for supervisors it is a necessity.

You can acquire listening skills by practicing. Here are some helpful hints:

Ten Steps Toward Effective Listening

1. Come to every conversation with the intent of obtaining information, to acquire and understand the other person's message. At the end of the encounter,

ask yourself: "What was this person, or these people, really trying to tell me?"

2. Show your interest in the other person and the message through body language. Lean forward toward the speaker. Maintain eye contact. Retain concentration. Don't allow yourself to be distracted by outside influences. These movements and this attitude encourage the speaker to "open up."

3. Ask questions to clarify what is being said, but not so many questions that it interrupts the speaker's flow. Repeat the message, as you understand it, in different words and see if the speaker agrees with your interpretation.

4. When the other person is speaking, don't be thinking about what you want to say or waiting for an opening so you can "jump in." Concentrate on the speaker's remarks.

5. Take notes for future reference, but write down only the main points of the speaker's message. Excessive note taking can be a distraction that prevents the message from coming through.

6. Get a good vantage point from which to see and hear. Positioning is particularly important in meetings. You want to hear everything that is being said. Also, be sure to obtain a copy of all material that is passed out.

7. Seek the essence of the message. This skill requires the most practice. It requires mentally sifting through extraneous material to learn what the speaker really wants to say.

8. Observe the speaker's manner and delivery. How important is this message to the speaker? Is he or she emotionally committed?

9. Make a mental summary of the message when the conversation is over.

10. Practice the foregoing suggestions in every encounter with another person or group at every level. You'll become the best informed supervisor in the company.

How to Listen to Instructions

The supervisor's job is to take instructions from senior managers and pass them along to line employees. That makes the ability to understand instructions the single most important skill a supervisor can possess. Nothing is more embarrassing (or career threatening) than getting something wrong and passing along an instruction that doesn't reflect management's intent.

Getting instructions right the first time, like most skills, is a matter of determination and practice. Here's how to do it:

1. Learn how to listen. Practice the suggestions on listening offered earlier in this chapter.
2. Be positive toward the instructions. Adopt a "can do" attitude.
3. Take notes as the instructions are given. Save comments for later.
4. Ask for clarification on any point or material that is not clearly understood.
5. On a step-by-step basis, repeat back your understanding of the instructions.
6. If an instruction is hazy, or poorly presented, it may be because the manager does not have a clear idea of what he or she requires. This happens frequently in business. It's up to the supervisor to probe and question until a clear requirement of intent is developed.

7. Don't be afraid to raise objections if concerned about how something will work. Be sure to offer alternatives as well.

8. When instructions from senior management are given verbally, write down your understanding of them and send this interpretation in a written memo back to the manager. This is the best way to avoid misunderstandings. It is also a good way to keep off the hot seat.

9. After the meeting is over, don't be afraid to call and ask questions as they occur. It is often difficult, however, to raise objections to a procedure after the meeting is completed.

10. Don't allow yourself to be bullied into accepting conflicting instructions from different senior managers. When receiving conflicting instructions, make both managers aware of the conflict and ask for a ruling on which takes precedence.

The supervisor who follows these suggestions will come across to senior management as someone with the right attitude who wants to get the job done properly.

HOW TO TAKE NOTES
YOU'LL BE ABLE TO UNDERSTAND THE NEXT DAY

The information is being fired out of a cannon at a manager's meeting. You are scribbling as fast as you can, but still always seem to be several thoughts and three paragraphs behind the speaker. The next day your notes seem to be written in Sanskrit. What to do? You can't take shorthand, and your penmanship would be better suited for the medical profession.

Here are a few tips for the supervisors who are still try-ing to make sense of their notes from that very, very impor-tant meeting held a few weeks ago.

1. Bring enough writing material to the meeting. That means at least one legal-size lined pad of paper and two pens in case one runs out of ink. (The backs of envelopes and a pencil stub that needs sharpening won't cut it.)

2. Write down the names of the attendees as they enter the room. If there's a roster, ask for a copy. The meeting hasn't even started and you've already acquired important data.

3. Write down the subject matter of each person's address as soon as it is announced. If there's a writ-ten agenda, get a copy.

4. Don't try to write down everything the speaker says—you aren't a stenographer—but concentrate on the major points of the address.

5. Don't bother with statistics and figures quoted by the speaker. This information is usually available after the meeting.

6. Concentrate on those parts of every speech that affect your department.

7. If displays such as graphs and charts are used, ask for copies. This saves you the trouble of scribbling down the information they contain.

8. If you miss an important point, wait until the speak-er summarizes. Often the same material is gone over a second time.

9. If a speaker is talking too fast, ask for the person to slow down. If material is flying past you, likely it's whizzing past others.

10. Finally, take along a pocket tape recorder with you as backup.

The person who follows these suggestions will be considered someone "who never misses a beat," at any meeting.

HOW TO GIVE INSTRUCTIONS

The first step in giving instructions to employees is to think through what you want done. Nothing makes the supervisor look more ineffective than a confused, incomplete, or incorrect set of directions given to line employees. Nothing assists a smooth transition into a new procedure more than carefully thought-out directions.

The best way to decide what needs to be done is to think the way systems analysts do. They *work backward from the result desired.* What they want out of a system determines what goes into it. Here are some of things to think about before issuing that first order:

What is the result I want in this situation?

What are the steps necessary to achieve this result?

Who are the employees best suited to carry out these steps?

What additional training, if any, do my employees need to carry out these steps?

How can the instructions be simplified so the employees will know exactly what to do?

Will these new instructions have an effect on any other phase of the department's operation? (This important consideration is often overlooked by supervisors when giving instructions.)

The next step is to actually give the instructions to the involved employees.

Make the instructions as clear and simple as possible.
Break them down into logical steps.

Tell the employees why these new instructions are being given. This is the best way to ensure their cooperation.

Allow for feedback from employees. Listen carefully to any objections or perceived problems.

Ask if the instructions are understood. Don't be impatient with employees who appear slow to understand. Perhaps what is being registered is discomfort with a new procedure.

Don't display pride of authorship. A line employee who does the job every day may have a better idea on how something can be accomplished.

Follow the results over the next several weeks to determine if things are going as expected.

Make minor corrections as needed.

Instructions Worksheet

Instructions Worksheet

Date_____

Result Required _____

_____

_____

Steps Necessary to Achieve Result

1. _____
2. _____
3. _____
4. _____
5. _____

6. _____

7. _____

8. _____

9. _____

10. _____

Employees Best Suited to Carry Out Tasks

<u>Name</u>	<u>Additional Training Needed</u>
_____	_____
_____	_____
_____	_____
_____	_____
_____	_____
_____	_____
_____	_____

HOW TO ASK QUESTIONS

I keep six honest serving men
(They taught me all I know):
Their names are What and Why and When
and How and Where and Who.

—RUDYARD KIPLING

Questions are the keys that unlock information. The supervisor who learns the art of asking the right question of the right person is the one who is better informed about what needs to be done and what is going on in the department.

There are many different types of questions. They include the following:

1. *Closed questions.* These call for a simple response, a "yes" or "no" from the person being questioned. A typical example is, "Did the shipment go out?"

2. *Challenging questions.* These questions often indicate displeasure. They are likely to put the person being questioned on the defensive, so they should be used sparingly. A typical example is, "Why didn't the shipment go out?"

3. *Questions seeking solutions.* These questions seek solutions or opinions from the listener. A typical example is, "What can we do in the future to make sure our shipments go out on schedule?"

4. *Open-ended questions.* This is a more expansive version of the solution-seeking question in that they allow the listener more latitude in framing a response. A typical example is, "How do you think we can overhaul our shipping procedures to make them more efficient?"

5. *Direction questions.* These are really questions phrased as orders. A typical example is, "Give me the total number of shipments that actually made it out the door yesterday."

6. *Choice questions.* These questions offer the listener a choice between two alternatives. They are often used to make a direction easier for the listener to swallow. A typical example is, "Do you want to work late tonight to catch up on this work, or would you prefer to come in early tomorrow?"

In many situations more than one type of question will be used to obtain the response, and information, desired.

The first step in framing any question is to decide what you want to know. This not only determines the type of question that will be asked, but whom you will ask for the information.

SIX GOOD QUESTIONS
THAT FIT MOST ANY SITUATION

There are "generic"-type questions that can be used in many business situations to help supervisors find out what's going on in the department and how things can be improved. They can be helpful when speaking to senior managers or line employees. What is more, when used properly, they can give the supervisor a reputation for being "incisive." This short list is golden. Tape it to the drawer of your desk and use as needed:

1. What kind of results would you like to see that you're not getting now?
2. How do you feel these results can be achieved?
3. What isn't working well? Alternate: What do you find is the biggest bottleneck?
4. What do you think needs to be done to fix things? What stands in the way of these changes being made?
5. What, specifically, can my department do to improve our performance?
6. What are your biggest concerns? What can go wrong? How can we guard against these possibilities?

Ask these questions from time to time, and you'll get more information and suggestions from your employees than you can absorb.

EIGHT WAYS TO MAKE LINE EMPLOYEES MORE EFFECTIVE COMMUNICATORS

Supervisors need to know what's going in within their departments. Nobody likes surprises. In fact, one of the ways to establish a reputation for being an ineffective supervisor is to occasionally present management with surprises.

The way to avoid surprises is by establishing a departmental communication system that keeps the supervisors on top of every situation. Line employees, however, often don't possess good communication skills. Many don't regard communicating with management as part of their responsibilities. ("I'm supposed to get today's orders down to Credit by 3:00 P.M., and I do it!") These employees must be taught the importance of communication and their role in providing necessary information. The supervisor is the teacher.

Here's a program that will make line employees more effective communicators:

1. Tell line employees *why* the requested information is necessary. This not only provides a reason for the request, it gives employees a sense of their value to the organization.
2. Be specific on what is required. If you're fuzzy on what is wanted, you'll get back fuzzy information.
3. Use preprinted forms whenever possible to make it easy for employees to provide necessary data. It's much simpler to fill in a blank line than it is to write a complete report from scratch.
4. Make sure that employees know how and where to obtain the data they'll need to provide the information.
5. Make sure the information is absolutely necessary. Many supervisors require volumes of data that are

never analyzed or even read by anyone. Employees soon learn when they're performing useless tasks.

6. React quickly when a report is late. Let the employee know that this tardiness is a serious matter. (Listen carefully if excuses are made. The "fix" may be somewhere else. Perhaps one employee didn't complete a report on schedule because someone else down the line didn't provide a necessary ingredient on time.)

7. Keep an open door. Employees must feel they can approach you with budding problems before they become serious.

8. Let employees know the information is being used and is appreciated. When appropriate, make comments such as, "Agnes, I see that you processed more than 200 orders last week. Good work! Our volume is growing. We may have to get you a faster computer."

TEN KEYS TO UNDERSTANDING OTHERS

Understanding is the ability to *comprehend*, to grasp the meaning of what is communicated. As all communication is between individuals, understanding others is a necessary skill for supervisors. Here are the keys for understanding the people, both senior managers and line employees alike, around you.

1. Listen carefully to what they have to say. Listening skills were discussed earlier in this chapter. Paying attention to what is said is the best way to get people to open up.

2. Remember what they said in the past. Experience is

a wonderful teacher. Some people are conservative in their remarks. Others exaggerate. The "track record" will tell you what to accept at face value and what to discount.

3. Assume that people are acting in their own self-interest. There's nothing wrong with this posture. Aren't you acting in your best interest?

4. Look for consistency. The consistent person is more likely to be reliable.

5. Place your faith in enthusiasm and passion. These emotions are more reliable gauges of sincerity than anything else.

6. Resolve to like the people around you. Make friends. People open up to those who like them. (They can't help but admire their good taste.)

7. Be open and candid. Never be secretive and hide things. People respond with openness to those who are open.

8. Don't be critical and judgmental. The quickest way to "shut off" someone is by being critical of their behavior or what they tell you.

9. Respect confidences. If something is said in confidence, don't repeat it to others. The person with a reputation for respecting confidences becomes a receptacle for information.

10. Be easy to reach and easy to talk to. Accessibility is one of the most important factors in receiving information.

<u>Six Barriers That Inhibit Understanding</u>

In the old movies many plots revolved around a situation in which a man and woman were absolutely crazy about one another but didn't get together until the final reel because of some colossal misunderstanding. What kept them apart? *A lack of communication.* The poor dears were all wrong about one another's motives.

Not properly understanding an employee or a senior manager is dangerous for a supervisor because it could result in misinformation. Here are six common barriers that inhibit understanding. Supervisors should guard against them.

1. *An assumption that the other person doesn't have anything important to say.* This is a very dangerous assumption and one with possible serious consequences for supervisors who don't pay proper attention to their staff members.

2. *An unwillingness to sift through extraneous material to get to the message.* Let's face it. Not everyone is a good communicator. It's up to the supervisor to help their employees learn how to organize and deliver information in a useful manner.

3. *A feeling that the message has been delivered before.* Supervisors sometimes tend to gloss over reports and data that appear similar to material received in the past. That's just the time when there's a golden nugget of absolutely vital information hidden on page twelve, paragraph four.

4. An *"I'm too busy" attitude that reflects impatience.* If a line employee delivering information gets the impression that the supervisor really has no or little time for this encounter, he or she may shortcut the message.

5. *Allowing interruptions during meetings.* The supervisor, meeting with an employee, who also handles phone calls, allows others to burst into the office, or looks at reports during the conversation cannot possibly get the full message.

6. *Ignoring facts that don't fit with preconceived ideas.* This is the most dangerous habit of all! Supervisors

who ignore the truth because they find it "uncomfortable" are destined to become more uncomfortable still.

SUMMARY

Precision in communication—conveying exactly what is meant—is very important. Even a small difference between what is meant and what is understood can lead to disaster.

Good communicators learn how to listen. They organize their own thoughts before trying them out on others. They speak and write simply.

Different methods of communication fit different situations. Supervisors should select the communication medium best suited for the occasion.

When reporting information to senior management supervisors should anticipate requests for additional data.

When reporting problems, always be prepared with a proposed solution.

In meetings, the key to effective note taking is to concentrate on the essence of the speaker's message.

The first step in giving instructions to employees is to carefully think through what needs to be done before issuing the first order.

When devising instructions to give employees, work backward from the result desired.

Questions are the keys that unlock information. The informed supervisor is the one who uses "who, what, when, where, why, and how" frequently.

To develop an internal information system, supervisors must teach their employees how to become effective communicators. The first step is to show employees why the information is necessary.

Understanding others is a necessary skill for supervisors.

Barriers that inhibit understanding include an assumption that the other person doesn't have an important or relevant message.

3

How to Speak so Others Understand

"The question is," said Alice, "whether you can make words mean so many different things."
—LEWIS CARROLL,
THROUGH THE LOOKING GLASS

The answer to Alice's question is a definite "yes." Words can mean different things to different people. The way people interpret what we say is just one of the factors that make accurate communication between individuals difficult.

HOW TO GIVE
VERBAL INSTRUCTIONS AND DIRECTIONS

Most of the communication between supervisor and employee is necessarily on a verbal basis. It's just not practical, or desirable, to put every order, every suggestion in writing. The problem, however, is that many times a simple instruction, request, or comment given verbally is completely misinterpreted by the listener. The supervisor is frustrated by the undesirable result, and the employee who believed that a direction was being faithfully followed is unhappy.

How to prevent, or at least reduce, these misunderstandings? The first step is for the supervisor to realize that care must be taken when speaking to line employees and senior managers alike. Be specific. Be precise. Any statement not thought through is likely to lead to unfortunate results.

Supervisors must also recognize that more "weight" is attached to everything they say simply because, to line employees, they represent authority. A statement that seems harmless can be blown out of proportion. (The higher the management level or title, the more important any statement from that person becomes. The president of any large corporation simply *cannot* make a casual remark without repercussions. On a plant tour the president of a big manufacturing company remarked that the shop floor looked "untidy." He was horrified the next morning to see every line employee busily engaged in clean-up—at the expense of that day's production.)

Supervisors must not only think through what they want to say, but consider how the message will be received and understood. They must even consider the likely reaction of the recipient. Here's a mental checklist to go over whenever speaking to a line employee:

1. What do I want to say in this situation?
2. To whom should this message be given? (How many people will be affected?)
3. If relaying information, do I have my facts straight? (Nothing undermines a supervisor's authority more than relaying incorrect information to staff members.)
4. How can I best word the message so the listener, or listeners, will understand it?

5. Will they get it the first time? Should the message be repeated?

6. What is the likely reaction of the listener? Will there be opposition?

7. Should the message be "packaged" to get the reaction wanted?

8. If giving instructions, is hands-on demonstration required? What needs to be done to set up this demonstration? Who will give it?

9. Does the person or persons receiving the instruction need to practice? For how long?

When reviewing this mental list, it is obvious that supervisors must carefully "construct" their verbal messages and instructions before giving them to employees. It is a responsibility that "comes with the territory."

Just as important as content is the manner of speaking. A message delivered in a loud voice or angry tone will be received negatively by the listener. Count on it! The anger will carry far more impact than the actual words used. *The reaction to emotion is almost always emotion.* Expect the listener to react angrily. When speaking in this manner, just be sure that displeasure with the listener is the message you wanted to get across. (Which means that an angry tone or loud voice should be used rarely, if ever at all.)

An important factor that should be considered when delivering a verbal message is *where*, exactly, will the delivery take place? The supervisor's office is the most secure point from which to deliver a message. It is the strongest symbol of the supervisor's authority. A new set of directions, a change in procedures, a problem that needs to be addressed, a reprimand to an employee—all are examples of situations in which supervisors might choose their offices as meeting sites.

There are many occasions when it is more appropriate for the supervisor to stop at an employee's desk or office. The employee may be in possession of the data that will be discussed. The supervisor may not wish to interrupt the employee's work. Stopping at a subordinate's office or desk is also a good idea when you wish to praise that person or show special recognition.

The supervisor may wish the exchange to appear casual. A message or instruction given to an employee when passing in the hall, or in the lunchroom, is just about as casual as you can get.

Meeting rooms may be required when directions or instructions are delivered to a large number of employees. Holding meetings away from the work area means the message won't be interrupted.

No matter how precisely you speak or how carefully words are chosen, an employee will sometimes get a meaning from them that is not intended. As Alice pointed out, words can mean a great many different things. The education of the employee, the region or origin, the employee's intelligence and training may all play a factor in understanding. That's why it's important to always ask for verbal feedback. Be suspicious of a short "okay" or head nodding from the listener. Did he or she fully understand the instruction? What was that instruction? If the employee is turned "loose" to follow the instruction, what happens next? The supervisor may be shocked to learn how many times the message gets "twisted."

As stated earlier, tone and manner are important communication tools. Directions must be delivered firmly. There must never be any question that the instructions or directions will not be followed. The employees deserve an explanation when given instructions so have a full one available. Be candid. Questions should definitely be allowed. Objections should be heard. Don't have pride of authorship. Give experienced employees credit for knowing their own jobs. Any suggested revisions from employees that produce the desired result more efficiently should be considered.

It is one thing to deliver instructions and directions that are clearly understood; it is quite another for the employees to have any enthusiasm for them. This is particularly true when instituting a new set of procedures or a different system. Supervisors must understand that people resist change. They prefer the familiar. Change is uncomfortable.

That's why it's important for the supervisor to display a positive attitude when giving directions. The *worst* approach is, "Here's another damn fool idea from those idiots upstairs in their ivory tower." *Never be apologetic when giving directions.* It is the business of management to try to improve things. Never blame management for making changes. This doesn't work because employees consider supervisors to be part of the management team. The supervisor must adopt the attitude that the changes are necessary, that they are for the better, and that they will be made to work.

Employees deserve an explanation of how the changes will affect them and the way that they work. Make this explanation as thorough as possible. Don't try to sugar coat a change that you feel the employees won't like.

When giving verbal instructions, the supervisor must also anticipate the likely reaction from staff members. What objections will be raised? How can these objections be answered? How can petty complaints be separated from legitimate concerns? Is someone on the staff more likely to complain than others? How can this person be "neutralized" at the meeting?

It is also important for supervisors to try to instill a team spirit. Use "we" instead of "you" when outlining new responsibilities. Ask for suggestions on how goals can be accomplished. The supervisor can demonstrate dedication

to making the changes work by personally taking responsibility for part of the job that no one else wants
        Morale-Building Hint: *Do some of the dirty work your-
self to win staff support.*

How to Receive Verbal Messages

You are consciously practicing "listening" to senior managers, peers, and line employees, so what else do you need
to know about receiving verbal messages? Quite a bit! Let's
assume that you're all attention whenever another person's
mouth is opened, and words pass over the lips. Here are
some additional tips:
1. Think about how the speaker uses words. Are they
   used in the same way you use them? What are the
   differences?
2. What is the speaker's emotional state of mind?
   Something said in anger or when tired may have a
   different meaning than the same words said when
   calm and rested.
3. What emotion or reaction is the speaker trying to
   get from you? What is the speaker's motive? Are
   you being manipulated by a senior manager? Is an
   employee trying to gain favor?
4. What is the speaker's track record? Does the speaker know what he or she is talking about? Does the
   speaker often try to manipulate people? Do the
   facts appear correct? Does the speaker often shoot
   from the hip? What is the speaker's credibility?
5. Is the speaker articulate? Some people have difficulty delivering the message they intend. Does the
   speaker need help in getting a point across? (The
   supervisor is often required to provide communication assistance to line employees.)

This kind of analysis will help the supervisor get more "truth" out of their verbal communications with others.

THE DANGERS OF VERBAL COMMUNICATIONS

Speaking to someone when passing in the hall or calling on the telephone is much simpler, more direct, and certainly less formal than writing a memo or letter, so why not use verbal communications to deliver almost all messages? The reason is because there are certain dangers associated with verbal communications. These dangers include the following:

1. Once the message has been delivered, it is lost in the air forever. The only record exists in the minds of the speaker and listener or listeners. It can be difficult to reconstruct exactly what was said, the tone that was used, or even if the message was ever delivered. Careers have been altered by the differences in memories over a message.

2. A written communication carries more weight, and therefore more authority, than a verbal message. It just seems more formal.

3. The verbal message is subject to interpretation. ("Yes, I heard you, but I thought you meant—.")

4. The verbal message or direction is more likely to be questioned. A written communication offers fewer opportunities for objections.

5. The verbal message is often delivered without thinking it through. The mere act of writing something down requires thought and organization.

All these problems don't mean that verbal communication should be discarded in favor of written messages. Nothing would ever get done. Knowing that the dangers exist makes it possible to guard against them.

Six Poor Speaking Habits

Humans begin speaking at about the age of one year. At two, the toddler is putting words together in very simple sentences. With such an early beginning at communication and long practice, it seems a surprise that many of us have poor speaking habits, but we do. Here are six of the most common:

1. We don't think through what we want to say. That often results in poor organization, a jumbled message, and even delivering messages that were not intended.

2. We don't choose words carefully. The incorrect word will convey the wrong meaning. This is just sloppy organization. It isn't necessary to have a large vocabulary to choose the right words.

3. We often don't consider the listener's possible reaction to what we say. We don't spend the time to learn their interpretation of our remarks. *We don't ask for feedback.*

4. We don't choose the proper time and place before we speak. Someone passes in the hall and the message is blurted out. Timing is almost as important as content.

5. We don't speak clearly. Too many of us mumble, slur words, let sentences trail off, don't face the listener, have poor habits such as distracting body movements, or otherwise fail to command the listener's attention.

6. We aren't interested ourselves in what we have to say. The speaker convinces the listener through his or her own passion.

These six habits are handicaps to effective communication. Do you plead guilty to any one of them?

WHY VOICE AND E-MAIL ARE OVERTAKING THE WRITTEN MEMO

In the modern office there is a computer terminal and what amounts to a telephone answering device at every work station. These devices are changing the way people in business communicate. For one thing, companies are eliminating personal secretaries except at the highest executive levels. For another, they are making the delivery of information a whole lot easier. Want to deliver a message to someone in another department who may be out of town? Call his extension and leave your observations on voice mail. When he calls in to his extension, the messages will be played back. Want to order changes in your department? Write up what you want done and send the information to subordinates electronically via computer E-mail. The computer keeps a record of the message in case you wish to refer to it later.

These devices spell the demise of the written memo as the preferred method of communication. Supervisors who don't know how, or are reluctant, to use them will find themselves as obsolete as carbon paper.

HOW TO CONDUCT A BRIEFING

A briefing is a meeting in which a detailed plan of action is revealed to employees. It is an important time because the success of the plan may depend on how well the details are communicated. What the supervisor wants to accomplish at a briefing is

1. To tell the employees why the plan is being instituted.
2. To give employees an overall view of how the plan will work.

3. To detail each employee's part of the program and to make sure that he or she understands it.

4. To generate enthusiasm for the plan through personal attitude and by accenting the positive aspects.

5. To demonstrate through organization and advance preparation that the supervisor, and therefore the company, is "on top" of the program

6. To offer an opportunity for employees to ask questions and raise objections.

7. To leave no doubt that the plan will be put into place. (Some supervisors with a sense for drama ask their employees to "sign off" on the program.)

Long before the briefing begins, think through how each of these goals will be accomplished. This requires advance preparation.

Here's a worksheet that will assist in that preparation:

Briefing Worksheet

Briefing Worksheet

Subject of briefing _____

_____

Date_____   Time_____

Attendees _____

_____

_____

Reasons for program _____

_____

_____

How program will work _____

_____

_____

_____

_____

Possible Objections

<u>Objection</u>   <u>Response</u>

_____   _____

_____   _____

_____   _____

_____   _____

_____   _____

_____   _____

_____   _____

_____   _____

_____   _____

Each employee's part of the program should be part of a separate worksheet that is given to the employee during or after the meeting. This worksheet, which details each person's responsibilities, is rather simple to create. Here's a sample:

Employee Briefing Worksheet

Date_____

Name_____   Department _____

Job Title_____

Program_____

Overall Objectives _____

_____

_____

_____

New Responsibilities

1. _____
   _____
2. _____
   _____
3. _____
   _____
4. _____
   _____
5. _____
   _____
6. _____
   _____

Training Required

1. _____
2. _____
3. _____
4. _____
5. _____
6. _____

                    Signed_____

In many companies no new plan can or should be implemented before obtaining a "sign-off" on the details from senior management. There's no point in putting something in motion and then later being second-guessed by someone from the executive suite. The corporate culture will determine how much freedom the supervisor has in instituting new procedures.

When developing the detailed procedures, work backward from the result desired. Think through the various steps necessary to achieve that result. This involves not only thinking about the tasks required, but who will accomplish them. It means lining up employee capabilities and training with job requirements.

Briefings go more smoothly when trusted subordinates are involved in working out various details of the program. Let them present these details at the briefing. *Using several individuals in the department to make presentations shows internal support for the program.* It also gives the supervisor the opportunity to observe employee reactions as the presentations are made. Be sure to go over the material that subordinates will present to make sure there are no surprises.

HOW TO RUN A BUSINESS MEETING

The meeting room for the briefing should be large enough to comfortably accommodate all the attendees. Be sure to reserve the room in advance. Provide writing pads and pencils for those who wish to take notes. Check out the sound system. Make sure that other props, such as overhead projectors, video equipment, and so forth, are in the room and working.

Arrive at the meeting room early. When the employees file in, note the seating location of those who may be opposed to what is being presented. You may wish to check their reactions to your presentation. Start the meeting at the scheduled time even if a few people are late. This is one important symbol of a no-nonsense session.

Set an agenda with so much time for each presentation. Always put a "fudge factor" into the schedule as some presentations will inevitably run overtime. Act as a moderator to make sure that questions and comments from the audience don't throw the schedule out of whack. (You want to allow time for questions and comments, but don't allow them to take over the meeting.)

The agenda should include scheduled short coffee and "relief" breaks in the morning and afternoon. A break for lunch is also necessary. One problem with breaks is that it is always difficult to get people back into the meeting room. Always begin again on time even if some people have not returned. They won't be late after the next break. For a very busy agenda, lunch can be brought into the room. Providing coffee and soft drinks in the room shows thoughtfulness

How the employees are *addressed* is a matter of choice and the size of the audience. When the audience is large, supervisors will often stand behind a lectern or podium, facing the crowd; if the audience for the briefing is small, supervisors may opt to sit with the employees at a large table, adopting a more informal and "folksy" approach.

At all times, be candid with the employees. If the plan is intended to correct a problem, say so. If it means additional work, longer work hours, cutbacks, or other hardships, say so. Employees should be told that senior management is behind this plan. Finally, when discussing the details, don't discount the possibility that someone in the audience may come up with a better mouse trap. If an employee has an idea or a method that will better accomplish the desired objective, consider it.

These suggestions are specifically aimed at briefings.

TEN TIPS TO MAKE
A BUSINESS MEETING A SUCCESS

1. Think twice. Have a good reason on for holding the meeting. Useless meetings, or those with marginal

agendas, are probably the single biggest time waster in American business. Before scheduling a meeting, ask yourself: Is the reason for this meeting urgent enough to take employees away from their normal duties? Never call a meeting so you can listen to the marvelous sound of your own voice.

2. Set a specific agenda with a timetable. Remove all fat from the subjects to be discussed.

3. Invite only those with a keen interest in the subject matter. Otherwise, people with no "investment" in the material may feel free to wander from it (and take others along in the process).

4. Give attendees advance notice of the subjects to be discussed. This makes them better prepared to make a contribution.

5. Prepare the meeting room. Make sure the space is adequate and the seating arrangement is as desired, that the props work, that refreshments will be brought in on schedule, that writing material is available, and so forth.

6. Run the meeting on schedule. If there are guest speakers, set a time limit for them. Moderate questions from the floor so they don't take over the meeting. Don't allow people to delay the meeting by returning late from breaks.

7. Encourage audience participation. Ask questions. Solicit comments. This is the best way to keep their attention.

8. Make the presentations lively. Use audiovisual aids, props, surprises, changes of pace, and so forth to keep the audience's attention.

9. Provide a written summary of what was discussed. That means someone must be appointed to take notes. The summary should include a list of those

who attended the meeting. Give a copy to all attendees.

10. List conclusions reached at the meeting and the requirements for future action. List each attendee's responsibilities for those actions.

A Business Meeting Checklist

The following checklist will be helpful when setting up a business meeting.

Business Meeting Checklist

Business Meeting Checklist

Date of Meeting _____

Subject Matter_____

Number of Attendees_____

Names of Attendees _____

_____

_____

Attendees notified of meeting?   Yes_____   No_____

Meeting room arranged?   Yes_____   No_____

Location_____

Props needed _____

_____

Sound system checked?   Yes_____   No_____

Visual equipment checked?   Yes_____   No_____

Seating arrangements_____

Agenda prepared?   Yes_____   No_____

Refreshments arranged?   Yes_____   No_____

Material and equipment required_____

_____

_____

Others making presentations _____

_____

Making Presentations to Senior Management

Any presentation to senior management is nervous time. Management often judges the abilities of supervisors based on the impressions they make during presentations. No one wants to look foolish or unprepared. Here are some hints that will make those nervous time presentations go smoother.

1. The purpose of most presentations to management is to transfer information. They'll want to know the results of some task you've been given. Be sure to have the information available that management requires—and have it in a form that is easy to understand.

2. Prepare for the presentation. Rehearse what you want to say. *You're on stage.* Get the material down pat.

3. Use visual displays, graphs, charts, and so forth to make the material easy to understand.

4. Anticipate the questions you may be asked. A thorough, thoughtful response to a question is impressive. Some experienced presenters even set up situations that naturally lead to certain questions for which they are well prepared.

5. Be prepared to reach conclusions and make recommendations. This is part of a supervisor's responsibility.

6. Prepare pass-outs and other material that summarizes your presentation.

7. Be brief. Senior management wants the bottom line. Don't take too long to get to it.

8. Be candid. Don't try to hide bad news. ("What must be revealed eventually should be revealed immediately." Henry Kissinger.)

9. Know every detail of your operation, but don't get lost in these details. Management wants the big picture.

10. Don't wait around for applause. Get out of the room when the presentation is over and the questions are finished. If management wants you to stick around, they'll ask.

How to "Sell" Your Proposition

Most supervisors do not consider themselves sales oriented. Some may even harbor a dislike for the sales personality. Yet every manager at every level in every corporation must be a salesperson at least some of the time. The selling is internal. Supervisors must "sell" their employees on good work habits and safety. They must sell dedication. They must sell a sense of common purpose. They must sell every new program that comes along. Their sales effort is both upward and downward, to line employees and senior management alike. (Senior management must be "sold" on the idea that the supervisor's department is in good hands.)

In business management, internal selling means getting others to accept your ideas. The art of the sale is to influence someone else to "buy." In this instance the buyer is buying a proposition. How can supervisors who have never been exposed to sales training or techniques learn how to influence others and sell propositions? Use the following tips to influence others:

1. *Present ideas simply.* People don't buy what they don't understand. However, be thorough. The higher the level of management you're trying to sell, the more thorough you must be.
2. *Use enthusiasm and passion in your presentation.* People are influenced by emotion.

Career Hint: *The supervisor who can get senior management enthusiastic about a proposition is the supervisor destined for promotion. Learn how to sell management.*

3. *Talk straight.* Speak true. Answer questions and objections fully. Mean what you say. Never obscure the truth. People at all levels respond to honesty.
4. *Consider the well-being of the buyer.* Don't propose anything that works against it.
5. *Talk about the benefits.* Good salespeople do this all the time. It means tailoring a proposition to the self-interest of the buyer. Talking about the benefits to senior management might include how a proposition might cut costs, reduce time, or improve bottom-line profits.
6. Don't sell or be "on stage" all the time. Management and employees alike would find this behavior tedious. Pick your spots.

Follow these suggestions, and you'll become the best internal salesperson in the company. Who knows? They may give you a territory and a quota.

THE ART OF ANSWERING QUESTIONS

The supervisor is supposed to be the "answer person," someone employees can come to with questions about the job, the company, procedures, changes, even personal matters. Senior management expects supervisors to have ready answers regarding daily work flow, the progress of a project, the morale of employees, bottlenecks, and a host of other things. In fact, many supervisors find that most of their time is spent answering questions. Those who learn how to handle questions make their jobs much easier. Here are some tips for mastering this "art."

1. Listen to the question all the way through. Ask yourself, "What does the questioner really want to know?"

2. Know your own job and the jobs of your employees. Learn all the details of every job in the department. Most of the questions coming from employees are job related.

3. Know what's going on in your area of responsibility. (You'll have to establish an internal communication system to be adequately informed.) Most of the queries from management are for information related to status of work in process and various projects.

4. Anticipate the questions people may ask. You'll be better prepared with answers.

5. Think carefully before you answer. Just because an employee wants an immediate response doesn't mean you should give one. A careless answer may create unforeseen problems.

6. Be thorough. Be sure to fully answer all questions.

7. Don't "wing" answers. If you don't know something, say so and find out. Giving incorrect information makes you appear incompetent. It's a career killer when done to senior management.

8. Don't speak for other departments. Many times employees have questions regarding health bene-

fits, insurance, and so forth that really should be answered by the Human Services group. You may think you know the answer, but the question should really be referred to the proper people.

9. Don't deliberately provide misinformation. If a line employee asks you about something that is confidential, decline to answer rather than mislead.

10. Don't tell tales out of school. Don't provide information that the company has asked you to keep confidential. Does the person requesting the information have a right to it?

How to Handle Objections

When giving out work assignments to employees, installing new procedures, making any kind of change, or even when making propositions to senior management, supervisors can expect objections. They are a fact of corporate life. Employees will have all sorts of reasons as to why they can't possibly do whatever they have been asked to do. Senior management will recognize all the flaws in proposed procedural change. Learning how to deal with objections is a skill every supervisor must acquire. Here are a few tips that will help:

1. Listen carefully to the objection. Don't interrupt the speaker until he or she is finished (unless the same ground is covered over and over again).

2. Act pleased that the objection was raised. Treat it as an opportunity to clear up or review a point.

3. Refer to objections as "questions." This makes them less of a barrier to reaching an agreement.

4. Repeat back the objection as you understand it. ("You can't print the pick slips in the morning because you don't receive the inventory status report until later in the day?") Repeating an objection not only shows you understand the concern, it has the effect of deflating its importance.

5. Write down the objections. This further deflates their importance and inhibits the raising of still more objections when these have been answered.

6. Sort out the legitimate concerns from those that are based on resistance to change. The person who doesn't get the inventory status report in time to meet another deadline is voicing a legitimate objection.

7. Anticipate objections and prepare answers for them. This is particularly important when making presentations to management. Think about the possible concerns of management. Do you have answers for these concerns?

8. Don't be evasive or resort to half-truths. Answer objections candidly. By telling the complete truth, employees and management will both gain respect for you.

9. Recognize that *not all objections need to be answered.* Many positive things about a situation may more than compensate for a single negative point.

10. Never answer an objection in a smug, self-satisfied manner that suggests an important point has been scored in a debate. Use a soft, pleasant voice and glad-we-could-clear-this-up attitude.

How to Deal with Interruptions

Wouldn't it be wonderful if we could work without interruption until one task was completed before going on to the next? How efficient this would be! How much more could be accomplished! Unfortunately, that's not the way things work in most companies. The supervisor must deal with questions from subordinates, phone calls, brush fires, emergency meetings, command performances from senior management, and a host of other distractions. How to handle these interruptions and still keep the normal work load on track is a problem that plagues every supervisor. Here are some tips that will help you cope:

1. Come into the office or plant early. The first hours in the morning are when the fewest interruptions occur. Working late is another option.

2. Don't allow employees to walk into your office at their whim. Of course you must be accessible to your people. Schedule specific times when you will be available. Make sure all employees know when these times are.

3. Shackle the time-tyrant sitting on your desk. What tyrant is that? The telephone! People will interrupt a conversation with someone who has been waiting an hour to answer any phone call. When in an important conference, put your phone on phone mail. Return calls when you have time.

4. Obtain advance copies of all meeting agendas. If the subject matter isn't related to your area of activity, or if your presence hasn't been commanded, don't attend. Also leave meetings early when the subject matter strays from matters that concern your department. You won't be missed.

5. Focus on what is important. That is, establish priorities. Be sure that all employees in the department understand these priorities. Don't allow yourself, or others in the department, to be interrupted or distracted by trivial issues.

6. Be neat. After being diverted by a problem it's often hard to remember where you were. An organized approach to your work will help you find your place.

7. Be cautious about interrupting others. If you respect their priorities, they will respect yours.

8. Delegate responsibilities. Give your people power. If you don't trust others to make decisions, people must come to you for everything. What a waste of time!

SPEAKING BEFORE LARGE GROUPS: HOW TO STOP BEING AFRAID

It is one thing to talk to a few employees in your office or across a table in a small meeting room and another to address a large audience from behind a podium. Public speaking is a terror that makes many people nervous. Will they remember what they want to say? How will the audience receive the message? Is the presentation convincing? Can they handle questions and interruptions? Will everything go right?

Everyone dreads looking the fool. For the novice speaker, there's good reason for the fear. We've all agonized and fidgeted while one of our peers has botched a presentation.

The best way to avoid anxiety is to *stop being a novice*. Practice speaking before groups at every opportunity. Practice in front of your spouse and relatives. Bore them stiff, but keep at it. Join an organization such as Toastmasters that has programs for novice speakers.

How to Prepare for a Speech

The success of a speech depends on the preparation that goes into it. There are those who can get up on a moment's notice, "wing" a speech, and wow an audience, but the practice isn't recommended for the beginner. Here's how to prepare:

1. Have something worthwhile to say. This is the first rule of all speechmaking at every level. If your message isn't important, why have you risen to speak?

2. Learn something about the audience. What would they like to hear that you know?

3. Do your homework. One of the things that can disconcert any speaker is a dispute from the audience over a remark. Avoid stating things that can't be proven. Know that you're right.

4. Write down the important points of your speech on 3" x 5" cue cards. These cards can easily be concealed behind a lectern or podium. They will be a comfort to you, even if you have the speech memorized.

5. Practice before anyone who will listen. Ask for comments. Be able to give the speech in your sleep. Practicing also gives you an idea of how long the speech will run.

6. Include anecdotes and examples to illustrate important points.

7. Get to the place where you'll make the speech well ahead of schedule. You can use a few minutes to relax and go over your cue cards.

How to Make a Speech

The preparation is completed, you're at the podium, the audience is eyeing you suspiciously, wondering if a boring few minutes are ahead, and someone signals you to begin. The moment of truth has arrived. What now? Here's how to make a speech:

1. Put your cue cards on the podium. They are your lifeline in case you drift.
2. Pause and take a deep breath. This will help you relax. Don't speak too quickly. You won't lose the audience by starting slowly. When you do begin, speak up.
3. Look at various people in the audience. If someone you know is present, try to establish eye contact.
4. Don't read the speech—there's nothing worse; deliver it.
5. Use a delivery that is natural for you.
6. Use language the audience will understand.
7. Pause whenever you like. The audience will wait for you.
8. When using graphs, charts, and other displays, make sure the audience can see them. Also make sure these displays emphasize the points you wish to illustrate.
9. Be brief and to the point. If nothing else, the audience will be relieved.
10. Allow time for questions from the audience. Anticipate what the questions may be.
11. Repeat the questions. This procedure makes sure the audience has heard them and gives you a few precious seconds to come up with a reply.
12. When the speech is finished and the questions are over, sit down. You've done it!

EIGHT MISTAKES OF NOVICE SPEECHMAKERS

Now that you know what to do when standing before an audience, what should you avoid doing? Avoid these common mistakes made by beginning speakers:

1. Do not force a style that is unnatural for you, such as telling jokes when you lack a sense of humor.
2. Do not race through the material as if you want to get "off stage" as soon as possible.
3. Don't present the material in illogical sequence so that you lose the audience.
4. Do not use a monotone or a dull delivery that puts everyone to sleep.
5. Do not use technical terms and obscure language that only a few in the audience understand.
6. Do not lack conviction, which means you can't convince the audience.
7. Do not let your presentations wander without making any significant points.
8. Do not seem bewildered by questions and ill-prepared to answer.

EIGHT TIPS GUARANTEED TO MAKE YOUR SPEECH A SUCCESS

You can avoid all the mistakes, do everything right, and still deliver a speech that causes nothing but yawns. Here are the secrets the real spellbinders employ to capture their audiences:

1. They engage the emotions of the audience. The emotion can be love, hate, a desire for salvation, or whatever, but the spell binders make people *feel*.

2. They're passionate themselves about the subject matter, and this passion is transferred to the audience.

3. They're self-assured while speaking. This confidence is felt by the audience.

4. They seem to genuinely like the audience. The audience reciprocates. (It's hard not to like someone who likes you.)

5. They have a sense of drama and build each speech to a climax.

6. They address the self-interest of the audience, something all good salespeople do.

7. They seem to be speaking to each person in the audience individually.

8. They "speak to the back row." Everyone in the audience can easily understand them.

KNOWING THE AUDIENCE

Speeches must be tailored to fit the audience. A speech delivered to line employees should not contain the same material as one delivered to senior management. The two groups have different interests, and the first rule of speechmaking is to make the talk interesting. Before putting together a speech learn something about who will attend, ask yourself four questions:

What are their interests?

What would they like to know that you know?

What do you have to say that would benefit them?

What are their *expectations* from this speech?

The size of the audience is also important. A speech given to an intimate group seated around the table should employ a different delivery style from one made in a crowded auditorium.

How to Use Cue Cards and Other Memory Joggers

The human brain begins to function well before birth. It continues to operate during an individual's lifetime, whether that person is alive or asleep, right up to the moment when he or she rises to make a speech.

—Sir George Jessel
Industrialist

Nothing is as embarrassing as standing before a large, expectant audience with a mind that has suddenly been wiped clean as a freshly erased blackboard. It is an embarrassment that has happened to almost every speaker. To avoid it, many speakers use cue cards and other memory joggers to help them remember.

Cue cards are simply 3" x 5" note cards on which the speaker writes important points to be covered. Collectively, they are a summary of the speech. The cards can be carried in a coat pocket and are easily concealed by a podium or lectern. The speaker *doesn't read to the audience from the cards*, but uses them as a reference. When the cards are numbered they also help the speaker know exactly where he or she is in the speech. When compared to the elapsed time, they provide a gauge as to whether to speed up, slow down, or keep at the same pace.

Using visual displays also helps the speaker remember the material to which the display refers. One glance at a graph can release a flood of thoughts. Slides, in particular, are excellent memory joggers. They carry the speaker along a defined path.

Don't be ashamed of using these devices. The object of a speech is to transfer information from the speaker to the audience. They're more interested in the material being presented than whether you needed a little help delivering it.

Speech Checklist

To make sure all bases are covered, novice speechmakers can help relieve their nervousness by filling out the following checklist before delivering a speech.

Speech Checklist

Date of Speech_____

Location_____

Topic _____

Kind of Audience_____   Size _____

Audience's Interests_____

_____

_____

Allotted Time_____

Important points to cover_____

_____

_____

_____

_____

Anticipated questions _____

_____

_____

_____

_____

Displays needed _____

_____

Pass out material?   Yes_____   No_____   Type_____

HOW TO MAKE CERTAIN THE AUDIENCE UNDERSTANDS WHAT IS BEING PRESENTED

The speech seems to be going smoothly, you're hitting on all cylinders, the important points are being covered, brilliantly, you think, but how can you be sure the audience understands what is being presented? *Are they getting it?* In most instances it is difficult to stop the presentation and ask for feedback, so how can you be certain? Here are a few clues:

1. Watch the audience. Do they appear interested in what you have to say? A bored expression is a powerful hint that the message is not getting through. So is a restless stirring.

2. Pause in the presentation and watch what happens. Does the audience seem anxious for you to go on? Do they begin to talk among themselves? If they're talking they may not be getting it.

3. Are people walking out on you? The reason why may be obvious.

4. When asking a question of the audience, is it difficult to get a response? Maybe they don't understand what you want to know.

5. After the presentation is completed, are there very few questions from the audience? They may not know what to ask.

Every one of these situations suggests the audience may not fully understand what is being presented. Of course, another explanation that fits each of these situations is that the audience *does* understand, but they just aren't interested.

HOW TO USE HAND-OUTS TO MAKE SURE THE AUDIENCE TAKES THE MESSAGE HOME

One of the despairs of every speaker is that audiences retain so little of what is presented. Good speakers understand this and try to emphasize only one point or two. Try to cover too much material and all will be lost. One way to ensure that some of the more important points of a presentation will be retained is to provide pass-outs that the audience can take home or back to the office with them.

Pass-outs are very popular with audiences. They serve as memory reminders and hard-copy proof of attendance. The pass-outs should not be word-for-word written copies of the speech, but rather summaries of what was presented. Copies of the visual displays are popular because people like illustrations. Don't overwhelm the audience with material. They're more likely to take home a single sheet than several dozen pages.

One word of caution about pass-outs: Don't make any material available until after the speech is completed. If you do so members of the audience will be looking at it rather than listening to what you are saying. Arrange to have the material placed on tables just outside the meeting room shortly before the speech is completed. People can pick up copies on their way out.

WHAT THE AUDIENCE REMEMBERS

If the average audience doesn't retain much from a presentation, what, exactly, are they likely to remember? Here's a short list:

1. They remember passion and enthusiasm. What moves you will move them.
2. They remember surprises. Tell them something they

don't expect to hear.

3. They remember the stuff that's repeated over and over. Reinforce the important points you wish to make.

4. They remember what benefits them. Always address the self-interest of the audience.

HOW TO GET FEEDBACK FROM THE AUDIENCE

There's nothing more awkward than completing a presentation, asking the audience if there are questions, and receiving a stony silence. (Of course, that is feedback of a kind. The audience is telling you that you bored them stiff.) Here's how to ensure feedback from the audience.

1. Ask for it. Start the presentation with something like, "This talk is going to be about_____. I hope the information will be useful to you. When I finish, maybe I can learn something from you. What I want to know is the following_____." Everyone in the audience will be making mental notes as to what to tell you when it's their turn.

2. Pass out question cards. Members of the audience who are reluctant to speak up may be willing to make a comment in writing.

3. During the question period following the presentation, praise several of the early questions. ("That's an excellent observation. Let's follow it and see where it leads.") Others in the audience may want to bask in the same praise.

4. Never ridicule or downgrade any question. You're inhibiting others from opening up.

5. If the audience appears to be reluctant to ask questions, start the ball rolling by asking questions of them. It's surprising how often this works.

SUMMARY

Words mean different things to different people. The way people interpret what is said is just one of the factors that complicates communication.

Supervisors must not only think through what they wish to say, but consider how the message will be understood by the listener.

The method, or manner of delivery is just as important as the content of the message.

Directions and orders must be given firmly. Never be apologetic when giving directions.

Employees deserve an explanation of how changes may affect them and the way that they work.

When listening to another person speak, consider not only the context of what is said, but how the speaker uses words.

One of the dangers of verbal messages is that there is no historical record of what was said, except in the minds of the speaker and listener.

Many people don't think through what they mean to convey before beginning to speak.

Voice mail and E-mail will soon overtake the written memo as a popular form of business communication. Supervisors must not be reluctant to use these mediums.

A briefing is an important test of communication skills. The success of new procedures depends on the thoroughness with which briefings are conducted.

The single most important factor in the success of a

business meeting is to have a good reason for calling one.

Most supervisors are nervous when making presentations to senior management. The jitters may go away once the supervisors fully understand that the purpose of most management presentations is to transfer information.

Supervisors must learn how to sell both line employees and senior managers. The way to sell is to present things so they appear to be in the "buyer's" best interests.

Both line employees and senior managers expect supervisors to be prepared to answer questions concerning departmental activities.

Objections are a fact of corporate life. Learning how to deal with them is a skill that every supervisor must acquire.

Deal with interruptions through better organization, scheduling time better, delegating authority, and screening phone calls.

Practice talking to whoever will listen to master the fear of speaking before audiences.

The most common error of novice speechmakers is to adopt a style that is not natural to them.

Good speechmakers engage the audiences' emotions through their own passion.

Use pass-outs as one way of ensuring that the audience takes the message home.

4

How to Write so
Others Understand

*The blank sheet of paper is God's way of telling
me just how hard it is to be God.*
—(SUFFERING SUPERVISOR TRYING TO THINK OF
WHAT TO WRITE IN A MEMO TO THE BIG BOSS.)

WHY SUPERVISORS NEED
TO ACQUIRE WRITING SKILLS

Some supervisors with excellent verbal communication skills
are intimidated when it's time to put something in writing.
The written word seems more important somehow. It is so
formal, so final, *so open to criticism.* The blank sheet of paper
is a threat. What to say, and how to say it?

Supervisors must recognize that written communications
represent an important part of their responsibility. There's no
way it can be ignored. Take the time to acquire this skill. Like

any other skill, it is one that improves with practice. Here's an easy and obvious hint: *To become comfortable writing, write often!*

Why do you need to learn how to write well? The major reason is that writing so others can understand will help you do a better job.

In business, the purposes of most writing are as follows:

1. To communicate information
2. To communicate ideas
3. To issue directives, orders, and instructions
4. To make observations
5. To issue rebukes or offer praise
6. To make or accept offers and requests
7. To detail problems
8. To make proposals and suggest improvements

Supervisors will find that at some time or another they will be required to provide written communications in each of these categories in the form of memos, letters and reports.

How to Present Ideas and Other Material in Writing

When staring at that blank sheet of paper *the first thing to think about is your purpose.* What, exactly, do you want to communicate? What message do you want to send the reader, or readers?

Let's assume you wish to write a memo to employees about a forthcoming fire drill. If you have a problem constructing such a memo, begin by scribbling down what you wish to achieve. Your notes might look something like this:

1.Let employees know there will be a fire drill.

2.Tell them why it will be held.

3.Give them the day and time the drill will be held.

4.Provide instructions on what to do during the drill.

Once the purposes are clear, the memo practically writes itself. Here's what the completed memo might look like:

Date_____

To: *All Employees*

From: *Frank Overboss*

Subject: *Fire Drill*

Local safety regulations require us to practice periodic fire drills. Such a drill will be conducted, Tuesday, December 12, between 10:00 and 11:00 A.M. The signal that the drill has begun is three short horn blasts over the intercom system. When the alarm is sounded, all employees *must take the following steps:*

1. Turn off all office equipment.

2. Leave your work area.

3. Go to the nearest fire exit and leave the building.

4. Report to your section head in a designated area in the parking lot.

5. Remain outside the building until the clear has sounded (five short blasts).

6. Return to your work area.

No one is exempted from this drill. If you do not know the location of the nearest fire exit or the assembly area outside the building, contact your section head immediately.

Frank Overboss

WHAT'S IN A MEMO

The memo we've used as an example is clear and to the point. It contains the typical elements found in most instruction type memos. These are

What is to be done.

Why it is to be done.

How it will be done.

Memos should be confined to a single subject. They should be short, clear, and, of course, accurate. (If the writer reversed the alarm with the all-clear signal, there's going to be one confusing fire drill!)

Memos should also let the reader know what response is expected. In the case of the fire drill memo, the employees aren't required to make a written response. Another kind of memo making an inquiry, for example, might require the reader to answer. *If you need an answer, make sure the memo asks for it.* ("Joe, please get back to me on this by the end of the week.")

Memos to senior management will usually contain information or make requests. Others are "for the record." Let's face it, many memos are written as protection, to make sure that management is aware that a problem couldn't be helped. ("We didn't get the packing done on schedule because our supplier was late delivering the cartons.") They're easy to recognize because the sender usually copies everyone in the building. Keep these kinds of memos to a minimum. They come across as alibis.

Memos are also informal. They normally don't include titles. They make a point, give a direction, ask for, or give, information in as few words as possible, and they are finished. There's nothing wrong with a one-sentence memo if tence memo if it makes the point that needs to be made or a one-word reply to another's memo.

Some individuals are memo happy. They write to everyone in the company. Every day forests of trees are cut down to provide the paper for their memos.

Career Hint: *The degree of attention your memos receive is inversely related to the number of memos you send.* Those who send memos at every opportunity, including situations when a phone call would do, find that their communications are ignored. Be sure that what you have to say is important and that a written memo is the proper way to say it.

WRITING MEMOS THAT GET ACTION

Many memos sent to line employees seem to achieve no result at all. The directions given by the supervisor are ignored. It's as if they never had been written. How can you be sure that written directions will be followed? Here are several suggestions:

1. Make the memo clear. Let there be no mistake about what is intended.
2. Use positive rather than negative directions. For example, don't put out a memo stating that, "Employees must punch in before 8:00 A.M." Say instead "Employees must punch in before 8:00 A.M."
3. Be firm. The memo should clearly show that the supervisor expects the direction to be carried out.
4. Match directions to capabilities. Don't give directions to employees who don't have the experience or skill to carry them out.
5. Allow enough time. Don't send a flurry of "lightning bolt" memos that demand immediate action at the expense of current assignments.

WRITING MEMOS TO TOP MANAGEMENT

Are your memos to the brass frequently ignored? Do they seem to disappear without a trace into the cosmos? Here's how to get attention when you send something upstairs:

1. Cut the amount of correspondence by at least two-thirds. Senior management only wants to hear from you if things are going wrong, or if you have an extraordinary thing to say. Don't report the commonplace unless specifically directed to do so.

2. Keep the memos short. One page is better than two, a few sentences better than several long paragraphs. The shorter the message, the more likely it will be read.

3. *No matter what the problem, never say in writing that the job can't be done.* Senior management may agree with the assessment as it refers to you personally and bring in someone else to do it.

4. Make it simple for management to decide and reply. For example, when outlining a problem, suggest alternative solutions. ("We can do A, or we can do B. What do you recommend?")

5. Don't send surprises up the ladder. Senior management doesn't like it. If the news is really news, telephone ahead with a verbal assessment before the memo gets upstairs.

HOW TO USE OUTLINES TO ORGANIZE MATERIAL

Making an outline before beginning the actual writing can be helpful to the supervisor in written communications, particularly when constructing reports, or when the material will be lengthy. Outlines are useful for

1. Clarifying the important issues
2. Organizing the material
3. Making sure that the material is presented in a logical sequence
4. Making sure that all the important points are covered
5. Keeping the writer from "wandering" from the central purpose

The first step in preparing an outline is to define the purpose of your writing. Keep this definition to a single sentence. Reducing the message to a single sentence is a discipline that requires you to come to grips with the central issue of this communication. *If the purpose can't be defined in one sentence, it still isn't clear enough in your mind.*

Next, organize the material by putting it into logical sequence. Logical for whom? For the reader, of course! Begin by dividing the theme or central idea into three or four key thoughts. (Remember what we said earlier about an audience's ability to retain material? It's valid for reading audiences as well. Don't try to cram too many central ideas into one communication.)

These central points cover the important ideas you wish to present. If the presentation is a train taking the reader from point A to point B, the central points are the stopover stations.

The bare-bones outline format will look something like this:

I.
  A.
    1.
        a.
    2. a.
        b
    3.
  B.
    1.
  C.
    1.
        a.
        b.
        c.
II.
  A.
    1.
    2.
        a.
  B.
  C.
III.
  A.

The Roman numerals represent the key ideas in the report. The other numbers and letters are subheadings (or thoughts and facts) that fit under the key ideas.

Using an outline helps you arrange and rearrange the material before beginning the actual writing. It helps you determine just where things fit in the presentation, and perhaps even uncover a few things that don't apply at all. These latter subjects should be eliminated. Once the outline is completed, all that's left is "fleshing" out the presentation by filling in the blanks between the outline headings.

Sample Outline

Improving Productivity by Building New Plant (Theme)

I. Current Production System
  A. Method
    1. Advantages
      a. Machinery and plant fully amortized
      b. Low unit production cost
      c. Trained work force
    2. Limitations
      a. Inability to make changes
      b. High set-up costs
      c. High down time
      d. Mediocre quality
  B. Plant Location
    1. Long distance from markets and suppliers
    2. High local taxes
    3. Convenient for work force
II. Proposed Production System
  A. Method
    1. Advantages
      a. Improved output
      b. More versatile
      c. Uses new production techniques
      d. Addresses changing market conditions
    2. Costs
      a. Equipment investment
      b. Cost for retraining work force
      c. Plant moving costs
III. Conversion Problems
  A. Time required to convert to new system
    1. Learning curve
    2. Possible loss of market share
  B. Logistical problems
    1. Finding new suppliers

C. Personnel considerations
   1. Relocation costs
   2. Key employee defections
      a. Early retirement option

Each one of the subjects covered in the outline would require considerable expansion in the actual report. With the outline technique the writer has the opportunity to shift subjects to various sections to present the material in its most effective and logical sequence.

REWRITING, THE KEY TO EFFECTIVE WRITING

Nowhere is it written that you must dash off a single draft of the report and send it off to all those eager eyes waiting anxiously to read it. Good writers hone and polish their material. When they read over the material to themselves, they apply the following hard questions to it:

A. Will the audience be interested in what I have to say? (Unless the answer to this is positive, you don't have a good reason for writing the report.)

   1. Did I establish my theme?
   2. Did I get my central ideas across?
   3. Did the report progress in a logical sequence?
   4. Is the material simple to understand?
   5. Is the writing and language clear?
   6. Did I leave anything out that should have been included?
   7. Is there anything in the report that should be omitted?
   8. Is there anything in the material that could be misinterpreted?

Until you get the "right" answers to all these questions, keep polishing!

THE ESSENTIAL SELF-HELP
KIT FOR EVERY BUSINESS WRITER

Sidney Sheldon "writes" by talking into a dictating machine. For the rest of us, the following items will help our material look more professional.

1. *Legal-size lined note pads.* Keep note pads at the office and at home to jot down ideas as they occur. You never can tell when inspiration may strike. Note pads are useful for initial drafts and playing with central ideas. Nothing seems "finalized," and therefore changes are easier to make.

2. *A word processor.* Hear this through. You don't have to be computer literate to operate a word processor. Most advanced electronic typewriters now include word processing capabilities. These machines are easy to learn and inexpensive to buy. With word processing you can move ideas around as you see fit, and add or delete material (a word, a paragraph, a page) according to your whim. You see what you've written on a screen before anything is printed out. Many models even include programs that check spelling and grammar. In any kind of situation where the boss may ask you to make revisions, a word processor is invaluable.

3. *A good dictionary.* Don't go overboard and buy an unabridged dictionary, they're too unwieldy. Do get one that includes business terms.

4. *A thesaurus.* Have trouble thinking of the exact word to fit your meaning? A thesaurus will help you find it. *Roget's* is by far the most popular.

5. *A book on grammar and style.* One of the best is a slim volume titled *Elements of Style* by Strunk and White.

6. The most essential element in the self-help writer's kit is in the writer's head. Think about: what you want to say. Even for the dullest of internal memos, writing, is, after all, a creative work.

Identifying the Audience
for Written Material

One of the first things to consider when writing something is who, exactly, is likely to read it. The audience determines not only what you write, but the writing style. For example, a memo containing an instruction to line employees would contain a simple explanation for the instruction and step-by-step directions for carrying out the instruction. A memo or report to senior management might be more detailed, including the information to support any conclusions.

Memos to employees would be written as directions to be followed. Memos to peers would be written as requests. If the readers will be engineers, technical terms can be included. Before putting the first word to paper, consider the following:

1. Who will be reading this?
2. What is their current level of knowledge about this subject?
3. What do I want them to learn from this communication?
4. What reaction do I want from them?
5. How can I make the material clear to them?
6. If I need a response, have I made this need clear?

Writing Reports

A report is an information transfer, from the supervisor to management. They are necessary, they are time consuming, and they can be tedious. Supervisors, however, should not ignore how important reports are for career advancement.

SEVEN THINGS MANAGEMENT
WANTS TO SEE IN A WRITTEN REPORT

In any company, a supervisor's reputation is determined by two things:

1. How well the supervisor's department performs.
2. The supervisor's ability to communicate to senior management.

Keep the department humming and let management know what's going on, and a successful career is assured.

Verbal communications are certainly important, but written reports can establish, or wreck, a supervisor's reputation. The verbal remark is made and lost in the air. The written report is a document that remains within easy reach, a monument to the supervisor's ability—or the lack of it.

Here's what management wants to see in reports:

1. A clear statement as to what the report contains. This statement should be at the very beginning of the document. This allows managers to decide if they wish to read further.
2. A short report. The longer the document, the less likely it will be read completely.
3. A report that provides information in a format that is easy to read and simple to understand. If the report must contain technical data, it's all in one section so management can skip over it.
4. A report that provides documentation for claims and assertions. In other words, a report that is accurate.
5. A report that reaches conclusions and makes recommendations.
6. A report that summarizes the material.

7. Finally, and most important, a good reason for writing the report.

WHAT MANAGEMENT DOESN'T WANT TO SEE IN REPORTS

Reports that drive management up the wall, and think poorly of the report writer in the process, contain the following:

1. Too many pages. (Also too many reports. The more often you direct something to management's attention, the less importance is attached to each document.)
2. Technical terms, long sentences, imprecise language.
3. Fuzzy conclusions, equivocations, lack of recommendations.
4. Advertisements for yourself. ("Due entirely to my efforts we were able to cut production time on this product from three hours to twelve seconds.")
5. Long columns of figures.
6. Misinformation. This is a career killer. Make sure the facts are correct.

Here's a report worksheet to help you make sure all the important elements are included:

Report Worksheet

Report Worksheet

Subject matter _____

_____

Date due_____   Requested by _____

Copies to _____

_____

_____

Objectives _____

_____

_____

Methods for obtaining information _____

_____

_____

_____

_____

Draft of report (use as many pages as necessary) _____

_____

_____

_____

_____

_____

Displays _____

_____

_____

_____

Conclusions _____

_____

_____

_____

Action recommendations _____

_____

_____

_____

How to Simplify Writing

The most effective writing is the kind that connects the writer to reader. Connection is what all writing is about. This is accomplished by keeping the writing as simple and clear as possible. Here's a short list of do's and don'ts:

1. Define the message you wish to get across. Make sure this message is important.
2. Don't package too many ideas in a single memo or report. The more ideas contained in a document, the less likely that any of them will be retained.
3. Write simple, declarative sentences.
4. Avoid cliches and trite phrases.
5. Don't qualify every statement.
6. Don't confuse formality and stiffness with good writing. For example, why write, "It has been brought to my attention," when "I heard that" says the same thing in fewer words?
7. Read your own material. Do you believe what you're trying to say would be clear to others? If not, a rewrite is in order.

How to Write a Proposal

Every time a supervisor wants to add or replace equipment, change a system, or put on more people, the idea must be "sold" to senior management. Because these kinds of changes involve additional expenditures, management wants to know why they are necessary. The supervisor will usually make the request in the form of a proposal, which is nothing more than a sales pitch in written form. How well the proposal is presented determines if the supervisor gets the request.

Career Hint: *To get what you need to run your department effectively, learn to write proposals that sell management.*

A good proposal convinces management of the benefits of the proposition. It gets management excited enough to act.

THE OUTLINE FOR A BASIC PROPOSAL

Here are the ingredients that should be included in most proposals:

1. *Opening.* The reason for the proposal, or why you're bothering the brass. Example: "This proposal addresses the need for change in our invoice processing system."
2. *Statement of the problem or situation the proposal addresses.* Example: "We are currently processing 30,000 invoices a month. With our current system and work force, an average of 22 working days is required before each invoice is mailed to a customer."
3. *Statement of goal.* Example: "With additional capital equipment, the transaction processing time can be reduced from 22 to 14 working days."
4. *Statement of the goal's benefits.* Example: "A reduction of eight days in transaction processing time would:
   a. Improve cash flow.
   b. Reduce credit balances.

    c. Provide an early warning system for poor credit risks.

5. *Statement of bottleneck at the heart of the problem.* Example: "All information required to process an invoice is currently key entered, a manual process that requires 100 clerical hours a week. Sorting takes another 40 hours a week. When one of our entry or sorting clerks is absent, a backlog is created that requires heavy overtime hours to correct."

6. *Statement of Solution.* Example: "Optical scanners are available that can 'read' the original documents, saving the key entry step. The scanners also sort the documents, eliminating the sorting step. Installation of this kind of equipment would improve throughput by one-third, reducing processing time from 22 to 14 days."

7. *Statement of the price for the solution.* Example: "The monthly lease and operating costs for a scanner that would handle our documents are as follows:

Lease cost	$ 6,000
Maintenance	1,800
Operator	2,400
Supplies	600
Total monthly cost	$10,800

8. *Statement of the cost and/or time savings the solution would offer.* Example: "The monthly cost for our current manual data entry method is as follows:

Three key entry clerks	$ 6,600
Two sorting clerks	4,000
Key entry equipment	1,500
Maintenance	400
Supplies	600
Cost of current system	$13,100

Cost of proposed system	$10,800
Monthly savings	$2,300

9. *Statement of other benefits.* These are the benefits that may be more difficult to quantify, but may represent the real reason why management may consider the proposal. Example: "The eight days reduction time in processing will
   1. Improve cash flow.
   2. Reduce outstanding credit balances.
   3. Reduce bad debts."

(Note that these are the stated goals made earlier in the proposal. Proposals should always meet their stated objectives.)

10. *Statement of a wonderful future once the one system is in place.* Example: "The scanner we have researched will handle projected invoice volumes until the year 1999."

11. *Statement of the time needed to implement the system along with any special requirements.* Example: "Time required to install system and train staff is estimated at six months from time of approval. No facilities modifications are required, except for special wiring, which is an estimated one-time cost of $3,700.00"

What Not to Put into Proposals

Do not include statements in proposals that are subject to challenge. If, for example, the monthly lease cost for the scanner has not been verified with the vendor, do not include it. If one statement is questionable, the entire proposal is suspect.

(Hint: Never propose anything to management in which the cost savings are slim or the benefits are obscure. The people in the executive suite don't like close calls. Write proposals that overwhelm them with all the advantages.)

Constructing a Proposal from Scratch

Proposals must be special, and they must be specific. Most must be written from scratch, every bit of it original material. They can be intimidating. What can the supervisor who may not write well do to make the presentation to management appear professional? Here's a beginning:

1. Make sure you thoroughly understand the problem that requires a solution. Write it down. Let others you trust read what you've written. See if they understand and agree with it. Polish the writing until someone can read about the problem for the first time and understand *why it's a problem.*

2. Consult with others about your proposed solution. Is it the only one that makes any sense? Write the solution down and let others read what you've written to make sure that both problem and solution are presented clearly. Polish the writing until someone can read the problem, read the solution, understand both, and feel, "by George, that's the only way to go."

3. Ask people you trust to raise every objection they can think of to the proposed solution. Consult with people within your department about their concerns. Write down the valid objections. Find solutions for these objections. If one objection particularly bothers you, it will also bother the brass.

4. Collect information on all related costs. Verify all figures. Go over the arithmetic at least three times. (Obvious arithmetic errors will shoot down any proposal. Management will wonder about every other claim the proposal makes.)

5. Prepare a draft of the entire proposal. Go over it with people you trust.

6. Make changes as needed. Polish the writing to make sure it is clear.

7. Try out the finished proposal on a friend. Did the friend understand it?

8. Rehearse the proposal. Even though the proposal is written, most are presented verbally.

That will do it. Make your presentation to management. Proposal writing is like all good writing: a lot of soul searching, investigating, reviewing, polishing, and rewriting. The following worksheet will help make sure all bases are covered.

Proposal Worksheet

Proposal Worksheet

Outline of problem _____

_____

_____

_____

_____

Problem's bottleneck_____

_____

_____

_____

Costs associated with problem _____

_____

_____

_____

Outline of solution _____

_____

_____

_____

_____

Cost of solution _____

_____

_____

Time needed to implement solution _____

_____

Training needed to implement solution _____

_____

Goals and benefits of solution _____

_____

_____

_____

_____

Objections to solution _____

_____

_____

_____

Answers to objections _____

_____

_____

_____

Cost savings _____

_____

_____

Other tangible benefits _____

_____

_____

Future benefits _____

_____

_____

Other considerations _____

_____

_____

Copies of proposal to: _____

_____

_____

USING GRAPHS AND CHARTS
IN PROPOSALS TO MAKE THEM COME ALIVE

The key to writing successful proposals is to make them easy
to understand. Management must be excited by the possibilities the proposal outlines. To become excited, first they must
comprehend. There's a common mine field that lies in the

path of understanding. That mine field is the presentation of facts in the form of numbers. Figures and comparisons, which are often necessary inclusions in a proposal, can make for dull, and sometimes difficult, reading. What to do when figures are necessary to make your case? Whenever possible, liven your presentations by using graphs and charts. A graph or chart makes numerical comparisons more obvious. (See accompanying graph.) They make the numbers mean something.

							Widget Manufacting Company			
							Semi-Annual Sales Figures			
SalesPersons		**Jan**	**Feb**	**Mar**	**Apr**	**May**	**June**	**Total**	**Average**	**Percent**
Cindy	Sinclair	900	1,200	1,300	1,700	1,600	1,300	8,000	1,333	38%
Frank	Fairly	700	1,600	730	1,900	820	1,800	7,550	1,258	36%
Dave	Dawson	100	1,100	1,400	1,000	890	870	5,360	893	26%
Elizabeth	Adams	900	1,400	1,500	1,500	1,300	1,600	8,200	1,367	39%
	Totals	2,600	5,300	4,930	6,100	4,610	5,570	20,910	3,485	100%

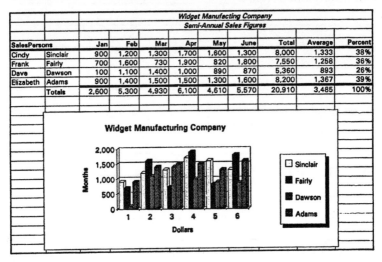

Presenting a Proposal to Management

The time has come to make your presentation to the brass. They want copies, but they also want to hear what you have to say. That's good. Any written proposal has a much better chance of being accepted if presented orally. So a time will come when you must be before the brass with your creation. Of course you're nervous. That's to be expected.

Here are some tips that will help you through this nail-biting time:

1. Try to limit the number of people in attendance. If possible, invite decision makers, but not their subordinates. (Fewer outside voices mean fewer objections and fewer distractions.) Of course, the managers involved in the decision must be present.

2. Present the proposal piecemeal. Hand out copies of the pages shortly after they are presented. If the complete proposal is given to management in advance, count on several people turning to the last page to get to "the bottom line." How can you keep them from skipping ahead? Have a staff member pass out the material section by section.

3. When making the presentation, be sure that agreement is reached on one point before going on to the next. Some people actually check off the section of the proposal once agreement is reached. If you're cursed with a sense of drama, check off each point on a blackboard.

4. If there's disagreement from management on a minor point that can be changed without damage to the proposition, make that change immediately. This "accommodation" shows that you are willing to make accommodations.

5. Follow up the presentation with a question and answer period. (Count on it—there will be questions.) Prepare in advance for the most likely questions. If you're a clever boy or girl, you may even lead the audience into asking certain questions for which you are well prepared.

6. Don't expect an immediate decision. Management will likely wish to mull things over. It's okay to ask for a commitment in terms of a decision date.

7. Resist the impulse to call the decision maker every day to see if anything has been determined. Your

reputation can quickly change from someone who has a grasp on problems to someone who is a pest.

8. Do offer to follow up to see if any later questions occurred to management long after the presentation was finished. Perhaps you have answers for latent objections.

9. Don't take refusal as a personal affront. There may be reasons that had nothing to do with your proposed solution to a problem.

10. Don't fight lost battles. If a decision is final, abide by it and try for something else another time.

WHY PROPOSALS SHOULD COME WITHOUT SURPRISES

Want to increase your chances of getting a proposal accepted? Management should be informed in advance when you plan to make a presentation. They should also be "spoon fed" information about what the presentation will contain. This will prepare them for what they will hear when you make the presentation. We all prefer the familiar to the strange, so give management the opportunity to become familiar with your proposition.

Giving management advance information on the content of proposals will also give you a chance to learn about possible objections and prepare answers for them. The fewer surprises presented to management, the better the chances of a proposal gathering dust inside a file cabinet drawer.

What you don't want to hear after a presentation is a statement such as, "Bill, I had no idea we were talking about this kind of money! Don't you realize how this scheme of yours would throw our budget out of whack?" The appearance is that you haven't done your homework.

How to Improve the Writing Skills of Line Employees

To do their jobs properly, supervisors rely on receiving a steady stream of information from line employees. They've got to know daily production figures, problem areas, how well new employees are settling in, if new procedures are going smoothly, and many other things. In short, they need to be on top of what's going on in the department. Where is this information available? From the employees who work in the department. That makes it important for the supervisor to teach line employees simple written communication skills. While it's unreasonable to expect supervisors to function as English teachers, there are a few things that can be done to improve the writing skills of their workers:

1. Make sure that the employees know exactly the kind of information that is required. Let there be no doubt concerning what you need to know and when you need to know it.

2. Make reporting as simple as possible. Provide forms with blank spaces to be filled in. Don't insist on writing if verbal communication will do. Never request a report that you may not read.

3. When reading memos from employees, concentrate on content rather than form. It's the information in the memo, not the grammar, that should be of primary interest to you.

4. Encourage employees to take night classes to improve their writing skills. If the company offers tuition support, make sure that all employees are aware of it. Offer advice on the kind of classes that would be of most benefit.

5. Go over with key employees some memos that have been written to you. Show them how they could have been improved. Stress simplicity. *Keep these sessions positive.* Never ridicule a poorly written memo.

6. Keep reference books such as a basic grammar, a dictionary, and a thesaurus in a handy place in the office where employees may refer to them.

7. Keep your office door open in the event any employee wants help constructing a memo.

8. Write your own memos simply and to the point. Let them serve as examples to your employees.

9. Be appreciative when an employee writes a clear, informative memo.

How to Write Letters to Customers, Prospects, and Suppliers

Letter writing is a chore that most supervisors wish would just go away. However, you will be required to write letters for many different reasons. Sometimes you'll need to respond to complaints from customers. Inquiries must be written to suppliers. Letters of authorization are necessary so vendors can proceed with projects. The thoughtful supervisor writes letters of congratulation to employees for noteworthy service or for certain personal accomplishments. All these situations, and others, require letter writing skills.

As with any kind of writing, the first step in business letter writing, before even pulling the paper out of the drawer, is to define the purpose. What is the message that needs to be conveyed? As with any kind of writing, the best business letters are simple and to the point. They say what needs to be said, and, mercifully for the reader, they end.

Never use a big word when a small one will do. Don't use technical terms unless absolutely necessary. Never look at the first draft of a letter and wonder what could be added. Instead, review your drafts with an eye for what can be deleted.

Important Rule of Business Writing: *The shorter the correspondence, the more likely it will get the desired reaction.*

Try to stay clear of the clichés and trite phrases that make most business letters a powerful sleep agent. Review your letters to make sure the meaning is clear. Take the time to rewrite when it is not.

The following are four sample letters which a supervisor might be required to write:

FOUR SAMPLE LETTERS

An Inquiry to a Supplier

Apex Office Supply Company
3344 Renault Road
Kansas City, KS 95182

Dear Supplier:

Please send me a written quotation with price, delivery and terms on thirty-six (36) reams of copy machine paper, your model #7655.

Cordially,

Edith Supervisor

Answering a Customer Complaint

Ms. Martha Mason
1121 Chocolate Rd.
Hershey, PA 91712

Dear Ms. Mason:

Your letter commenting that many pieces of broken walnuts were contained in a recent purchase of our one pound package of "whole" walnut meats has been referred to me. I'm sorry that this happened and regret any inconvenience it caused you. Let me assure you that our walnut meats are packed whole. Occasionally some pieces do get broken during shipping. This fall we are introducing new packaging that provides more protection.

Ms. Mason, thank you for taking the time to write to our company. I've enclosed a coupon that can be redeemed at your local store for a package of walnut meats.

Cordially,

Edith Supervisor

Praising an Employee

Mr. Richard Regular
5656 Bison Avenue
Lemont, NJ 90121

Dear Richard,

Congratulations on receiving an associate degree for completing the two year night study program in cost accounting at Claremont College. We're pleased when employees take advantage of the company's tuition reimbursement program.

I understand you finished fifth in the class. Considering you're carrying a full-day work load, that took real dedication and effort. It is the kind of dedication that gets noticed around here.

Richard, your efforts have made you a more valuable employee. Congratulations again on your achievement.

Cordially,

Edith Supervisor

Letter of Authorization

Victor Carlson
Bayside Waste Removal
3156 Watertown Road
Bayville, NY 87690

Dear Mr. Carlson:

This letter authorizes your company to remove the waste material from our Inglewood plant in accordance with the terms of your quotation of October 4. You should be receiving a formal purchase order from us within the next day or so.

When your truck arrives at our facility, please have the driver contact the plant manager, Harry Hill, for further instructions.

Cordially,

Edith Supervisor

These sample letters share several things in common:

1. They get to the reason for the correspondence in the first sentence.
2. They don't waste paper or the reader's time.
3. They don't wander, but stick with the purpose.
4. They get out after the message is delivered.

How to Respond to Customer Complaints

One of our sample letters was a response to a customer complaint. For supervisors who have this responsibility, handling an angry customer can be intimidating. What to say and how to say it? What words can put things right? Will saying the wrong thing only make matters worse? Here are a few suggestions when writing to unhappy customers:

1. Acknowledge the complaint very early into the letter. Do it in the first sentence if possible. Showing the complaint is understood reduces some of the customer's frustration.
2. Assume the complaint is legitimate. Never write to a customer with a statement such as, "We have never heard of this kind of problem."
3. If you know why the problem occurred, explain it to the customer. This makes the company appear more human. Remember, however, that explaining is not the same as excusing.
4. If it's within your power to correct the problem, correct it. If not, direct the problem to the proper level of authority.
5. Indicate that your company values the customer's business. This has the effect of deflecting anger.

One thing not to do is to ignore customer complaints or let them "age." This builds frustration and is one certain way to lose business.

SUMMARY

Written communications are an important part of a supervisor's responsibility.

The purpose of most business writing is to communicate information and ideas.

Before beginning to write, think about the purpose of the message.

Make memos short and clear; limit them to a single subject.

Making an outline before beginning the actual writing can be helpful in organizing material.

Effective writers polish their material. Take the time to rewrite to get things right.

Have a dictionary and thesaurus handy. If possible, use a word processor.

At the outset—before beginning to write—consider who, exactly, will be reading the message.

Most reports are an information transfer, from a lower level of management to a higher.

Keep reports short. The more pages in a report, the less likely the report will be read.

Connection between writer and reader is what writing is all about.

A proposal is a sales pitch to management. A good proposal gets management excited enough to take some action.

Make sure all reports and proposals contain accurate information.

Use displays such as graphs and charts to make proposals and reports come alive.

Even though proposals are written, many must be presented orally to management. These oral presentations can impact a supervisor's career.

Proposals should come without any surprises. Prepare management in advance for the key points contained in a proposal.

Help line employees improve their written communication skills by working with them, encouraging them to take classes, and by giving them a clear understanding of what kind of information is expected.

When writing business letters state the purpose of the letter in the first sentence.

Respond to customer complaints promptly. Acknowledge the complaint in the first sentence.

5

How to Train Employees

*Knowledge is the only Instrument of
Production that is not Subject to diminishing
Returns*

—J.M. CLARK

SELLING THE NEED FOR TRAINING

Training is like motherhood and the American flag: It's hard
to find anyone with a harsh word to say against it. Yet, in
many companies the "training" consists of a raw recruit being
shown the ropes for a day or two by a veteran employee and
then left to sink or swim.

Many supervisors find that senior management balks at
the expense and time needed to make a training program
effective. It is the supervisor's first responsibility to "sell" the
company on the value of a good training program. What's a
good training program? It's one that produces employees
who can handle their jobs without constantly needing assistance. Without a trained staff, the supervisor cannot
be effective

119

THE SUPERVISOR'S ROLE AS A TRAINER

Training is key to a supervisor's personal success. The well-trained crew that functions smoothly and delivers results month after month makes the supervisor look good. The equation is clear: Want a well-run department that's considered a model of efficiency? Set up a training program that teaches each person in the department how to do his or her job.

The problem is that many companies don't have a formalized training program. It's up to the supervisor to teach new people coming into the department what is required to handle their jobs. ("Here's Jane. Show her the ropes.") This challenge can be difficult for supervisors who have no experience in training techniques. Knowing what must be done and showing others how to do it are two very different things.

This chapter will help supervisors develop effective training methods. It will tell you how to put together a training program. You are the very first "student" in the program, the first person who will be trained. A good report card comes in the form of employees who will know how to do their jobs.

HOW TO DEVELOP TRAINING OBJECTIVES

The first, and most obvious step, in setting up a training program is deciding, exactly, what must be taught. What is the desired "product" of the training? One goal is obvious:

Career Hint: *The goal of all business training is to produce competent, self-sufficient employees who can function without constant supervision.* Does that sound like a simple goal? Think of all the employees who run to you day after day asking about things they should already know. Think of those employees whose work must be constantly monitored. Those employees weren't properly prepared for their jobs. Here are just a few of the things that must be learned on the road to self-sufficiency:

1. Knowledge of company policies and procedures and how the company operates.

2. Knowledge of the company's products, the customers the company serves and the company's position in the industry.

3. Knowledge of the specific job requirements, that is, the details of what the employee does and how he or she does it.

4. Knowledge of how the job fits into the company's method of operation. (This information is sometimes omitted. It's unfortunate because every employee has the right to know how what he or she does makes a contribution to the company. This attaches *worth* to their efforts.)

5. Knowledge of the reporting needed to provide timely information to supervision and management.

6. Knowledge of who's who in the company, not just supervisors and coworkers, but the movers and shakers in the executive suite.

That's a lot to learn, and trying to learn it all at one time can be overwhelming. That's another reason why the training must be carefully planned. It must be conducted at a pace that doesn't leave the trainee behind.

What's more, the learning process is never finished (which means the training job is never done) because there are always system changes, new requirements, personnel moves, shifting needs, different techniques, changing priorities, and, most important, retraining because *people forget what they know.*

To repeat something stated earlier, the first step in a training program is to develop objectives. How are objectives established? It's easy. Begin by asking yourself three very basic questions:

1. Who must be trained?
2. What must they learn?
3. What do they already know?

Looking at the answers to these three questions will give you a handle on training goals. Let's look at some common answers:

WHO MUST BE TRAINED?

All new employees.

Employees given different responsibilities.

Employees learning new equipment or systems.

Veteran employees transferring into the department.

Employees whose production has slipped.

The "what they must learn" list will vary by job description. Obviously, the same training is not appropriate to everyone in the department. Here's a typical list for various employee levels:

NEW EMPLOYEES

Background on the company, including who's who.

What the company does.

Company policies and procedures.

Reporting procedure.

Specifics of job.

Performance level that is expected.

Overview of department procedures.

Where job "fits" into department and company procedures.

Introduction to fellow employees.

EMPLOYEE SHIFTED TO ANOTHER RESPONSIBILITY OR TRANSFERRED INTO THE DEPARTMENT

Specifics of new job.

Performance level that is expected.

New reporting procedures.

Where new job "fits" into company and department procedures.

NEW PROMOTED

Basic management skills.

Motivational skills.

Leadership skills.

Specifics of new job.

Performance level that is expected.

Information and reporting level that is expected.

OBJECTIVES WORKSHEET

Training objectives then are primarily based on acquainting employees with the company and teaching them about their job responsibilities. The trick for the supervisor is to take these very general objectives and turn them into a specific training program. Here's an example of how to do it.

Let's take a new employee just entering the company and develop a customized training objectives list.

Sample Training Objectives Worksheet

Position:_____ File Clerk _____

Job Responsibilities	Training Needed
File documents and retrieve documents in file	Familiarization with filing system
	Familiarization with "route" to pick up documents for file
	Cross-reference location of documents
Microfilm documents.	Operation of microfilm equipment
Copy and fax documents	Operation of copy and fax machines
Prepare daily log	Familiarization with logging procedure

The objectives in the sample are restricted to job responsibilities only. A broader training objective for a new employee would normally include indoctrination and company orientation. (Sometimes the Human Resources Department will provide this basic information in separate training sessions before the new hire is "handed over" to the department.)

Use the following worksheet to develop training objectives for employees in your department:

Worksheet: Training Objectives

Name _____

Position _____

Job Responsibilities	Training Needed

TESTING EMPLOYEES TO DETERMINE WHAT KIND OF TRAINING IS NEEDED

One of the three basic questions supervisors must ask when putting together a training session is, "What does the person being trained already know?" To cite a simple example, the applicant hired on as a file clerk would not be able to handle these responsibilities without a comfortable knowledge of English and the alphabet.

What a person knows is often assumed, based on education and past experience. These assumptions can be dangerous. A diploma, or even an advanced degree, is no longer "evidence" of knowledge or job skills. Neither is past experience or a glowing reference from a former employer. Today's high school diploma certifies satisfactory attendance, nothing more. Employers, concerned about legal actions, give good marks to almost everyone who hasn't been caught with a hand in the petty cash drawer.

Lowered educational standards and former employers' reluctance to be candid mean that testing should be conducted of new employees to assess their knowledge and skill levels. This is particularly for those new hires just entering the job market straight from school. If this isn't done, there will be instances in which the instruction material will be over the trainee's head.

Career Hint: *Don't assume knowledge or skills on the part of new employees. Find out!*

What kind of testing is appropriate? Many companies still use intelligence or I.Q. tests, which, theoretically at least, assess an applicant's ability to learn. Don't set too much store by them. Recently, many so-called intelligence tests have been criticized for reflecting cultural biases. Leave these kinds of tests to Human Resources for assessing job candidates. (Let them deal with the complaints concerning their fairness.) The supervisor's concern is the level of skill and knowledge possessed by the new hire who has shown up for work bright and early Monday morning.

Skill tests measure the employee's ability to perform in certain areas. A typing test will demonstrate how fast and how accurately the applicant can type and nothing more. When the tests are used solely to assess training needs, there can be no complaint about them.

When setting up tests, try to construct those that closely imitate the actual job to be performed. (For the prospective file clerk, after explaining the filing system, put together sample documents to be filed or a list of documents to be retrieved. Check time and accuracy.)

The following worksheet may be helpful in determining what kind of tests are necessary.

Skill Test Worksheet

Skill Test Worksheet

Job Title_____ Department_____

Employee _____

Job Responsibilities _____

_____

_____

_____

_____

Skill Job Requires	*Has Skill Been Demonstrated?*
_____	Yes_____ No_____
_____	Yes_____ No_____
_____	Yes_____ No_____
_____	Yes_____ No_____
_____	Yes_____ No_____
_____	Yes_____ No_____
_____	Yes_____ No_____
_____	Yes_____ No_____
_____	Yes_____ No_____

ON-THE-JOB TRAINING

Someone once said that the best university is a tree stump with a wise man sitting on one end and a student on the other. It's an age-old example of one-on-one training and the transfer of knowledge. This method is used in business today whenever a veteran employee teaches a trainee how to handle a job. It is probably the most popular on-the-job training method of all. It is simple, direct, low cost and requires no planning. Many companies employ it to one degree or another.

Most on-the-job training is informal. The person being trained stationed at the work site with the supervisor or another person in the department who is familiar with the job to be done. The theory is that the experience and skill of the veteran will somehow be magically transferred to the newcomer.

Unfortunately, much of this kind of training is haphazard and incomplete. The new employee is "trained" as events occur. Exceptions that don't come up during the training period are not explained. Important information is sometimes omitted. Often, the veteran will continue to do the hands-on work and only allow the trainee to observe. At the end of the day, week, whatever, the veteran will look the trainee straight in the eye and say something like, "Okay, you should have a handle on this routine by now. Simple, ain't it? Any questions?"

The new employee won't want to risk looking like a dummy so the answer will be negative. However, he or she is left only partially "educated." There's important stuff about the job that hasn't been learned. That means mistakes, unsatisfactory performance, running to the supervisor every half hour, and "fill-in" sessions to make up for details that should have been part of the initial training program

As with any other kind of training, on-the-job training works best when there's a plan behind it. Planning starts with thinking through the requirements of the position. Here are the specific questions to ask when setting up on-the-job training for a new employee:

1. What, exactly, are the duties performed by the person with this job title?
2. How is the work performed? (Put the work flow in

logical, step-by-step order. In the process, you may learn how to improve it.)

3. What are the skills necessary to perform this work?
4. What information is necessary to perform this work?
5. Who is best equipped to provide the necessary information to the new employee? (Very often it is *not* the current holder of the job.)
6. How much time is needed for training?
7. Should the training be broken up into segments to make it easier to absorb?

The answer to these questions allows the supervisor to develop a specific training program. The following worksheet will also help.

On-the-Job Training Worksheet

Training Worksheet

Person to Be Trained _____

Trainer _____

Job Title _____

Duties _____

_____

_____

_____

_____

_____

_____

Work Flow Steps

1. _____

2. _____

3. _____

4. _____

5. _____

6. _____

7. _____

8. _____

9. _____

10. _____

Information necessary to perform work _____

_____

_____

_____

_____

_____

_____

_____

Time allocated to training _____

Number of sessions_____Dates _____

The completed worksheet becomes a guide for the trainer. In an actual training program, a different work flow sheet may be needed for every day of the week. The supervisor can use the completed worksheets to make sure "all bases were covered" during the actual training sessions. Even if different trainers are used for different portions of the training, the supervisor can be assured that all the material has been covered.

CLASSROOM TRAINING

Classroom training is appropriate when there are a number of people to be trained at one time. Companies with formal training programs often use the classroom system because it's easier, and more cost effective, to take the students to the teacher rather than the other way around.

There are two popular classroom training methods: (1) lecture and (2) workshop.

During classroom lectures students sit at desks and listen to someone talk at them. The planning that goes into this kind of training is usually more thorough. Other advantages include

1. The course material follows precisely what the instructor wishes to teach.
2. Traditional classroom teaching aids are available in the form of blackboards, printed material slides, movies, and so forth.
3. Guest speakers may be brought in to provide special expertise or relieve the main instructor.
4. It's relatively easy to administer written and verbal tests.
5. It's easy to maintain schedules.

CLASSROOM LECTURING

Classroom lecturing is an excellent teaching method for indoctrinating new employees, for equipment training, or when a new system will be introduced to a large number of employees.

The problem with lecturing as a teaching method is that it doesn't sufficiently engage the students. Just sitting and listening to someone speak for hour after hour is boring. As a result, there is frequently a low level of attention during classroom lectures. The material is flowing out the lecturer's mouth, but is it flowing into the students' heads?

WORKSHOPS

In the workshop training method students are given problems to solve. In most training workshops the problems are attacked by groups or teams. This system provides a competitive atmosphere that keeps the sessions lively. It is effective for seasoned employees to introduce them to problem-solving techniques. The instructor serves as overall group leader in guiding the class toward a solution. The students learn from the exercise, from other team members, from the instructor, and from rival teams.

Many companies combine training methods. They use classroom lecturing to indoctrinate new hires, send the rookies out in the work force for on-the-job training, and offer workshops for veteran employees when introducing something new.

SAMPLE CLASSROOM TRAINING SCHEDULE

One of the advantages of classroom lectures is that they can run on a strict timetable. More material can be covered in less time. Of course the schedule should be set in advance. The following is a typical schedule for lecture-type classroom training:

Sample Lecture Schedule

7:30–8:00   A.M.   Coffee, rolls, fruit

8:00–8:15	A.M.	Welcome and class introduction
8:15–8:30	A.M.	Overview of the course material
8:30–10:00	A.M.	History and organization of the company, using flip charts and overhead projector
10:00–10:15	A.M.	Questions and answers
10:15–10:30	A.M.	Coffee break
10:30–12:00	Noon	Company policies and procedures
12:00–1:00	P.M.	Lunch with company managers from credit, finance, production, and other departments
1:00–2:30	P.M.	Introduction to product line
2:30–3:00	P.M.	Questions and answers
3:00–3:15	P.M.	Afternoon break
3:15–4:00	P.M.	Product applications and demonstrations using actual products
4:00–5:30	P.M.	Work assignments for balance of week

The trainer must establish early on that the schedule means something. Pass out copies to the class as they arrive in the morning. Start on time. After coffee breaks and lunch, resume on time even if all students have not returned.

The Supervisor's Eight-Point Classroom Training Checklist

Want to start a training session by losing the respect of the class in the first five minutes? Begin by a wild search for a slide projector, an easel, chalk for the blackboard, a pointer, or any other material that should have been in the room before the training sessions began. The instructor also loses stature if the classroom is too small, or there aren't enough seats, or several of the students "weren't supposed to be there." All this confusion suggests disorganization.

The props and material needed for classroom training vary according to what is being taught. There are however, items common to most training sessions. The following checklist will help the supervisor ensure that no important item needed for presentations has been overlooked. This list is particularly helpful when the training occurs outside company facilities. (Because it isn't always easy to run out and get what you need.)

Checklist of Classroom Material

Checklist of Classroom Material

Proper size classroom   _____

Class roster   _____

Chairs and tables   _____

Coffee and rolls   _____

Soft drinks   _____

Lunch arrangements   _____

Lecture   _____

Chalkboard and chalk   _____

Easel and pad   _____

Slide projector   _____

Overhead projector   _____

TV and VCR   _____

Student pads and pencils   _____

Printed training schedules   _____

Demo equipment   _____

Power in training room   _____

Equipment supplies   _____

Printed student tests   _____

Guest speakers   _____

Printed training material   _____

Support people   _____

If the supervisor goes over this checklist a few days before class is scheduled to begin, there will be no awkward delays while someone races about trying to find an important ingredient in the training.

DISCUSSIONS, DISPLAYS, AND CLASS PARTICIPATION, THE KEYS TO LIVELY TRAINING SESSIONS

Want to bore employees to tears during a training session? Talk to them without interruption for hour after hour. Watch heads begin to nod and eyes glaze over. The way to keep students lively and attentive is by engaging their interest. Their interest can be engaged by changing the pace of the instruction. Here are some change-of-pace suggestions:

1. Talk for a time; then show a display.

2. Bring in guest speakers just so the students will hear a different voice and a different delivery.

3. Use different media such as television and slide projectors.

4. Ask "open" questions that stimulate class discussions.

5. Give demonstrations.

6. Arrange for "hands-on" periods when the students can get experience operating various devices.

7. Set up "teams" to solve problems. Arrange competition between teams.

8. Ask that students make presentations. (This is also a great way to silence those who talk in class. "The next person caught talking gets to give a presentation right now!")

9. Give short "pop" quizzes that aren't graded. Go over the answers in class.

10. Encourage questions from the class. When a question is interesting, ask other students for answers.

11. Have frequent short breaks.

SETTING UP THE CLASSROOM, A SEATING WORKSHEET

How the classroom is set up depends on the number of people in the class, the type of training, and the degree of control

Theater-Style Seating

the trainer wishes to maintain. Maximum control is maintained through theater-style seating, which consists of straight rows of seats with the audience facing the speaker who is usually on a raised platform. There is little audience involvement, no surface for the students to write upon, unless the chairs have an arm table, and no place to put papers. This style is suitable for large groups, orientation presentations, and straight lecture-type training.

When setting up this kind of classroom allow about six

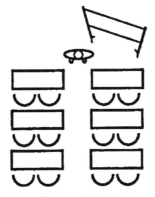

Schoolroom-Style Seating

feet for each person. The speaker will also require an area. Keep the presentation lively because this style of training is the one most likely to put students to sleep.

Workshop-Style Seating

For better group involvement, use the straight schoolroom style with each student allocated a desk or table for reading and writing. The desks can be set up in straight rows or in a herringbone pattern. The instructor is on the same level as the students. This section arrangement permits the instructor easier access to individual students and enhances the opportunity for two-way communication.

Allow about ten feet per student for either pattern. In the herringbone version, allow an extra side aisle down the middle. Another popular seating style is appropriate for workshops. In these workshops students are presented with problems. They break off into teams and attempt to solve them. Aside from offering practical lessons in the subject matter, workshops demonstrate the advantages of teamwork and cooperation.

The workshop arrangement requires large tables capable of seating all members of a team. Provide a sideboard where team members can obtain material used in solving their problems. Also provide blackboards for each team. The atmosphere can become competitive. Teams will be "jealous" about their solutions. Allow enough space between tables for privacy, and so the moderator can walk between groups.

What's the best kind of seating for your next training session? Obviously, it depends on the circumstances. The following worksheet will help you decide.

Seating Worksheet

Date_____

Training Session _____

Kind of Training (Check all that apply)

Indoctrination_____   Basic skills _____

Equipment_____   Job specific _____

Retraining_____   Other _____

Teaching method: Lecture_____   Workshop____

Schoolroom_____ Combined_____

Number of students in class_____

Size of available classroom:_____square feet

Equipment demonstrations: Yes_____ No_____

Audiovisual equipment needed _____

Number of speakers and trainers participating _____

Length of training sessions _____

Seating choice_____

THE VALUES AND DANGERS OF NIGHT SESSIONS AND HOMEWORK

Night sessions during a training class are dramatic evidence that training is a serious matter. They prove that the supervisor, by giving up his or her evening, is dedicated to teaching the students what they are in class to learn.

Problem-solving assignments, in which students apply knowledge that has just been learned, are often given during night sessions. During the evening trainees can work independently or in small groups, with the supervisor available for guidance. These sessions tend to be more casual both in dress and class format. They allow an opportunity for give-and-take between trainees and the supervisor. Homework assignments should also teach the students how to be resourceful, for example, where to go in the company to obtain information.

Don't use homework as a vehicle to teach students material that is not covered in class. You'll never know who "gets it" and who doesn't. Issue homework sparingly. You don't want the students to come into class so worn out from completing their assignments that they're too tired to learn.

Homework should not be so difficult or so "piled on" that the trainee feels overwhelmed.

The Value and Limitation of Written Tests

Announce a written test and expect to hear a groan from all trainees. No students want a test. Some supervisors don't care for them either. Do they have value? Can they help the supervisor make line employees become more productive?

One value for written tests is to assess what trainees coming into the company already know. That's why many training sessions *start out* with a test. It becomes an evaluation. Tests during and toward the end of the training help the supervisor determine what the trainee is getting out of the training. Is the material sinking in? Announced tests are also an implied threat that the trainee had better pay attention. Pop quizzes during the training tell the supervisor how well the trainees are keeping up with the material.

The disadvantage to tests is that while they reveal the people who really study and have learned the material, they don't necessarily prove the information will be retained. *Those who do well on tests don't always do well on the job.* Why is that? It's because tests in a classroom don't represent the real workplace. They don't show character, determination, or reliability.

A Chart That Shows Who Needs to be Trained and When

Outside of situations in which new systems are installed, in most departments the additional training of veteran employees is piecemeal. It is given where and as the supervisor thinks it is needed. This approach leads to oversights and inequities. Some employees are overtrained. Others do not receive the basic training needed to properly handle their job responsibilities.

Want an uncomfortable truth? *When an employee who has the ability to do the job isn't performing, it's the fault of the supervisor as much, or more, than of the employee.* So what is needed? Training programs that specifically target veteran employees! (Very early on in this chapter we commented that training is an exercise that never stops.) Once the conclusion has been reached that *everyone* requires additional training, the real questions become

1. What training do they need?
2. When should this training occur?

The answers, of course, depend upon the skills employees need to perform better.

The following skill assessment chart will help supervisors determine the timing and subject matter for follow-up training.

Skill Assessment Chart

Skill Assessment Chart

Job Title _____

Employee Name _____

Time in Position_____Tenure with Company_____

Other Positions Held _____

_____

Training Received_____

_____

Education Level _____

Special Classes _____

Performance Evaluation_____

_____

Job Requirements

Skill Required	Received Training	Proficiency	Needs Add'l Training
1._____	_____	_____	_____
2._____	_____	_____	_____
3._____	_____	_____	_____
4._____	_____	_____	_____
5._____	_____	_____	_____
6._____	_____	_____	_____
7._____	_____	_____	_____

Recommendations:_____

_____

Training Scheduled

Training class	Dates
_____	_____
_____	_____

Having such a chart for every employee in the department
would help the supervisor assess specific training needs
and set up training schedules.

How to Develop a Departmental Training Schedule That Doesn't Interrupt Production

It would be wonderful if everyone in the department could be bundled off to training sessions at one time, coming back a week or two later fully informed and really knowing how to handle their jobs. In the meantime, of course, the department would be shut down. There would be absolutely no production. The supervisor could go home. (One who set up that kind of schedule might be *sent home* by senior management.)

In the practical world, training must be scheduled so that it does not interrupt or interfere with the work flow. For example, setting up training classes during peak periods when every hand and body is needed to crank out the work is just poor judgment. If a department's production is not meeting standards, senior management is not sympathetic to the excuse that, "All my good people were in a training class." The supervisor who offered that alibi would be considered poorly organized.

That means setting up training for slack periods or/and on a rotating basis so only one or two employees is gone at a time. It's also important to make sure that backup people are available when key employees are in a training class. Want egg on your face? Send someone off to training class then learn that the backup person you assumed would be handling the job during the trainee's absence has a vacation scheduled for the same period.

Using the following worksheet will help the supervisor set up training at optimum times:

Training Schedule Worksheet

Training Schedule Worksheet

<u>Peak periods when no training should be scheduled:</u>

From_____ to_____

From_____ to_____

Employee	Training Needed	Training Available (Dates)	Job Could Be Handled by
_____	_____	_____	_____
_____	_____	_____	_____
_____	_____	_____	_____
_____	_____	_____	_____
_____	_____	_____	_____
_____	_____	_____	_____

Using this worksheet would assure the supervisor that not too many employees were trained at the same time. It would also assure that backup personnel were available to handle the employees' work assignments during any training period.

HOW TO TEACH NECESSARY WORK SKILLS

High school dropout rates in our major cities now average 25 percent. Between 20 and 30 percent of all U.S. workers lack the skills required to handle their *current* jobs. A large segment of the work force doesn't have the reading skills necessary to decipher an average instruction manual.

The biggest single problem facing business today is finding qualified workers. There are plenty of available bodies, but they are bodies without the necessary skills or training to do much of anything.

American industry is faced with the job of doing what the educational system has failed to do, namely, provide their employees with basic work skills. To be blunt, the job applicants coming out of high school today, and even those coming from some colleges, may not be able to read, write, or perform mathematical tasks well enough to handle most jobs. Who do you think will be saddled with the task of teaching the new work force these basic skills? Supervisors who have the responsibility for getting the work out with a poorly prepared staff, that's who. That means setting up training programs in basic skills before attempting specific job training. This will be a difficult task because few supervisors are teachers by profession.

Here's how to set up a basic work skill program on a departmental basis:

1. As part of the hiring process, test new employees on their basic skills. That means readin', writin', and 'rithmetic. (Don't rely too heavily on an applicant's diploma as proof of completed training. Today, for many schools, it's merely proof of satisfactory attendance.)

2. Make a list of the basic skills needed for each job function in the department.

3. Compare what you've got with what you need. (The skills new employees possess compared to the skills needed to handle the available jobs.)

4. From the comparison make a list of training needs.

5. Determine what training is available within the company to provide the needed skills. Send new employees to those training courses.

6. Make senior management in the company aware of the basic skills training that is necessary to have a productive work force.

7. Investigate the training available at local night schools, junior colleges, universities, and so forth that could provide the training needed to produce qualified employees. (Also, investigate the possibility of an "intern" program that would allow trainees to work part-time at the company while they attend classes to acquire basic job skills.)

8. Investigate the possibility of the company hiring part-time teachers from the local educational facilities to set up classes that can be taught at night on company premises.

9. Research company-paid tuition programs that reimburse employees for work-related training. (Human Resources can help you with this.)

10. Encourage employees to take classes to improve themselves. Be candid with them about the skills they need to succeed.

11. Offer recognition and awards to employees for completion of basic skills programs.

HOW TO TEACH EMPLOYEES GOOD WORK HABITS

In addition to failing to teach students to read and write properly, our schools are responsible for still another failure. They aren't teaching good work habits either. It is surprising, but many young people just entering the work force don't realize that they're expected to show up every day on time and give their employers "sixty seconds worth of distance run" for each and every minute. (After a payday the absentee rate in many industries rises dramatically.)

It's up to supervisors to instill proper work habits, particularly for new employees. No one offers a "work habits seminar," so for many supervisors it's difficult to know just where to begin. For one thing, "dedication" is a concept, not something tangible that can be touched.

Here are some ideas for instilling good work habits in all your personnel.

1. Set a good example. Nothing is more important.
   The supervisor sets the pace and tone for the entire

department. Work hard if you want line employees to work hard. (More on this "revolutionary idea" later in the chapter.)

2. Give employees a clear idea of what is expected. Every employee should know the company work rules and the kind of production output required of the job responsibility.

3. Provide good training. Spend enough time with new employees. Never rush through training or explanations. Show employees how to do their jobs well, and they'll be willing to devote more effort doing it. Employees who are unsure about what to do will often try to evade their responsibilities.

4. Watch how employees work. No, don't become a spy, but by observing how employees approach their jobs, how they handle details, and their general work habits, you'll be in a better position to offer suggestions for improvement.

5. Apply the same rules to everyone. Don't allow anyone in the department, even someone known to be a hard worker, to "goof off" or appear idle.

6. Be there, in the department, as much as possible. Make your presence felt, not only as the "boss," but as someone who is interested in helping each employee do the best job possible.

7. Acknowledge accomplishment and offer praise for good work. Give credit where credit is due. Recognition is a powerful motivator.

8. Keep an open door. Be available to answer questions. Be pleased when employees are concerned about their work.

9. Monitor quality and make quality a theme. Go over results with employees. Teach them how quality can be improved.

10. Have confidence in your employees. Give them responsibility. Make your confidence in your employees evident to everyone.

How to Retrain Veteran Employees

Retraining veteran employees is often touchy. Even the suggestion that retraining may be necessary is often a blow to their pride. Still, when performance slips, retraining is often a better solution than losing good people who have proven their worth to the company through past accomplishments.

There are signs that indicate when retraining a veteran employee may be useful:

1. When production from that employee is steadily decreasing
2. When the employee begins to make simple mistakes over and over
3. When the employee asks repeated questions about things that should be familiar
4. When the employee appears hesitant or unwilling to make simple decisions
5. When the employee finds excuses for anything that goes wrong
6. When the absentee rate from that employee rises dramatically

These signs suggest the employee has forgotten or is neglecting the skills that has made him or her a valuable member of the staff.

How can a supervisor retrain an "old pro" without damaging what may be a fragile ego? There are several ways to bring the old war horse to water.

1. Begin with an open policy that training in your department is a continuous process. There is no such animal as an employee who is "completely trained."

2. Classroom training is the easiest pill for the veteran to swallow. If classes are regularly scheduled, the veteran won't be offended because of being singled out for special handling.

3. Introducing the veteran to new equipment or a new system is another method that won't bruise an ego. Even the experienced employee recognizes that training is required when something new is introduced.

4. A frank discussion about the veteran's quality of work is useful if the supervisor is tactful during the meeting. Before the discussion the supervisor should gather enough "evidence" so there can be no dispute that the veteran's work is indeed slipping.

5. One other way is rather sneaky. It is to ask the veteran to help train a new employee. Of course this training will be overseen by the supervisor to make sure the newcomer gets proper instruction. In the course of developing and presenting a sound training program, the veteran is forced to review those basic skills that made him or her an effective employee. He or she is the recipient of the training even more than the rookie. (We said it was sneaky!)

HOW TO TRAIN VETERAN EMPLOYEES

When it is necessary to retrain a seasoned employee whose performance has slackened, the best procedure is to *go back to square one.* Review every procedure, every policy, every job skill needed just as if the old hand were a brand new employee. This may seem demeaning, but remember, you're trying to salvage the person's job *and keep the department running smoothly.*

TRAINING BY EXAMPLE, THE SUPERVISOR AS A ROLE MODEL

Whether the supervisor likes it or not, department line employees will copy his or her actions. They will behave the way the supervisor behaves. That offers a wonderful opportunity for indirect training. *Teaching by example is the single most effective method of training ever devised.*

To develop a dedicated staff, the supervisor must demonstrate dedication.

To produce hard workers, the supervisor must work hard.

If the supervisor is open and honest with employees, they, in turn, will be open and honest.

If the supervisor really listens to problems and complaints, employees will really listen when suggestions are made about possible improvements.

Employees will also copy negative behavior. If the supervisor is underhanded and deceitful, staff members will learn that "lesson" too.

What's the point of all this? To be a supervisor who is envied because of an efficient, hardworking, dedicated staff, be efficient, hardworking, and dedicated yourself.

How to Use In-house Professional Trainers

Supervisors who work for companies who have a staff of in-house trainers are lucky. The trainers are usually experienced professionals who use a variety of proven methods to teach necessary job skills.

Because of their past experience, trainers are also sometimes helpful in the recruiting process to find the best job applicants for available positions. However, supervisors should have the last word on the selection of line employees for their departments.

It's up to the supervisor to communicate with trainers concerning their needs. Tell them the skills and knowledge areas that should be emphasized during the employee's training period. Make sure the trainer understands all the requirements for the department and for the specific job. When the training is completed, get the trainer's assurance that the trainee can meet these requirements. You, not the trainer, have to live with the result.

If possible, meet with the trainer before any training begins. Provide a "laundry list" of the things you want covered. Be specific. Invite them into the department so they can see firsthand what your needs are. This communication is particularly important if the trainer has never met the person or persons to be trained.

It is also appropriate to ask for a report on the result of the training when it has been completed. Try to obtain both a verbal analysis from the trainer as well as a written report that becomes part of the employee's personnel file. If the company has a standard reporting form, accept that. A sample reporting form is illustrated later in this chapter.

Trainers are also helpful when installing new systems, or when assigning new responsibilities to a veteran employee. Again, you're going to get what you ask for so be sure to emphasize those skill and knowledge areas you want the trainer to cover.

Six Sources for Training Material

In many instances supervisors are handed total responsibility for training every employee who comes into the department. The deal is that the company provides the bodies and you are responsible for getting the work out the door. It's up to you to provide any training needed to make those "bodies" productive employees.

Help is available for supervisors facing this situation. There are a number of outside sources that can provide advice, training facilities, and material:

1. *Seminars.* Training seminars are available just about anywhere in the country. They're run by such organizations as the American Management Association and they are taught by business professionals with many years experience. The training can be costly, but it is much less expensive than the time and effort required to set up an in-house program.

2. *Journals and bulletins.* Professional management groups also publish a variety of bulletins covering many different business-related subjects. They address various training issues. These journals can provide a generic type of on-the-job training.

3. *Local educational facilities.* The colleges and universities in most towns offer evening courses on a variety of business-related subjects. Tuition rates are reasonable, and many classes are scheduled at night when they won't interfere with normal working hours.

4. *The local library.* Most local libraries are filled with books on business-related subjects—and

they're loaned out at no cost!

5. *Retired professionals.* Many retired pros would be delighted by the opportunity to teach what they know to a new generation of workers.

6. *Trade associations.* Many trade associations provide training material that is available to their members.

These are some of the inexpensive ways to put together a training package. Of course the material available from these sources is usually generic. It's up to the supervisor to tailor it specifically to the department's requirements.

SAMPLE STUDENT REPORT CARD

Report cards are useful for several reasons. When the company has a training department the supervisor will want to see the training results for any department employee who has gone through the process. When the supervisor trains, management may want to see a written report on each student at the completion of training.

What everyone wants to know is how effective the training has been and how well the trainee absorbed the material. Often, this report becomes part of the employee's personnel record.

When required to write such a report, be sure to cover all the bases. Give an honest appraisal of the trainee's performance. Here is a sample:

Student Report

Date October 15, 1993

Student Name Sandra Watly   Dept. Filing

Student Report (Continued)

Course:___Orientation, Basic Skills, and Job Duties_____

Behavior:___Sandra was punctual for all training sessions, was generally attentive, asked good questions, and displayed enthusiasm.

Assignments:___The assignments were turned in on time, were complete, and showed an understanding of the material. Some assignments appear to have been done in haste as they were a bit sloppy. However, they were above average.

Basic Skills:___This trainee demonstrated the basic skills necessary to handle her job assignment.

Quiz scores___83%___   Final Test Score___86%___

Comments:___Sandra is dedicated, intelligent, and likable and should make an excellent addition to the staff. She may find the routine of filing a bit dull. We should think about giving her additional responsibility once she settles in.

Signed _____

WHY TRAINING ALONE ISN'T EVER ENOUGH

The U.S. Military Academy at West Point has the most rigorous training program in this country. However, the real learning isn't accomplished in the classroom or on the drilling field. It's done in the dorms and halls where upperclass men teach the

In every kind of training there's a good deal that can be learned outside the classroom. There's more than knowledge that must be learned by the student for the training program to be successful. There is attitude. Knowledge can be taught by way of lecture and written material. The right attitude—a winning attitude—must be instilled.

How does the process work? It begins by the supervisor providing the right kind of example. The supervisor starts the day early; begins training promptly; has a plan in place; is organized, patient, and dedicated; knows the job to be done; and works a full day.

If this attitude is displayed strongly enough, *if the trainer believes in it*, it is absorbed by the new employees.

COMPLETE TRAINING CHECKLIST

Training, to be effective, must be complete. An inadequately trained employee will produce inadequate work. Don't just assume that everything has been covered in a training session. Confirm it. The following checklist will help the supervisor make certain that the training course has covered all the pertinent material.

Training Checklist and Worksheet

Employee _____Start Date_____
Job Title _____Department_____
Training Period _____

Orientation

_____   Company Policy and Procedures

_____   Work Rules

_____ Introduction to Company Personnel
_____ Personnel Records Completed

Basic Skills Assessment

_____ Reading Skills Assessment
_____ Writing Skills Assessment
_____ Arithmetic Skills Assessment
_____ Equipment Operating Skills Assessment
_____ Oral Communication Skills Assessment

Teaching Winning Attitudes

_____ Enthusiasm
_____ Reliability
_____ Dedication
_____ Flexibility
_____ Persistence
_____ Confidence

Teaching Job Responsibilities

_____ Outlining Daily Routine
_____ Explaining Work Flow
_____ Explaining Reports Required
_____ Explaining Reporting Structure
_____ Explaining Exceptions
_____ Explaining Company Management Chain
_____ "Hands-on" Teaching of Work Responsibilities
_____ Trial Runs Completed
_____ Where to Go for Help

Teaching Method Employed

_____ Coaching

_____	Telling
_____	Demonstrating
_____	Written Instruction
_____	Combination of Methods
_____	Classroom

Method of Evaluation

_____	Observation
_____	Oral or Written Testing
_____	Trial Runs

Instructor

_____	Supervisor
_____	Employee in Department
_____	Company Trainer
_____	Hired Outside Instructor

Reporting Training Results

_____	To Senior Management
_____	To Human Resources
_____	Department Files Only

SUMMARY

Training is key to a supervisor's personal success. In most companies supervisors find themselves responsible for the training of employees who work in their departments.

If the company doesn't have a good training program, the supervisor must sell management on the need for one.

The first step in an effective training program is deciding objectives. Make a plan. What is the desired "product" of the training?

The goal of all business training is to produce self-sufficient employees who can work effectively without constant supervision.

When developing training objectives begin by asking three basic questions:

1. Who must be trained?
2. What must they learn?
3. What do they already know?

Training objectives are based on the employee's job responsibilities.

New job candidates should be tested for basic skills because of deficiencies in our education system.

Companies must increasingly take up the role of teaching basic reading and writing skills.

Most on-the-job training is informal, with an experienced employee passing on information to a trainee. This method often leaves gaps in what the trainee needs to know to do the job.

On-the-job training works best when there's a plan behind it.

Career Hint: *To train someone to handle a particular job, break the job down into small, logical steps. Make each job responsibility as simple and clear as possible.*

Classroom training is easier and more cost effective for the company when there are a number of people to be trained. Classroom training is an excellent method for indoctrinating new employees or when a new system is introduced.

Workshop seating is best for problem-solving training sessions or when the students will be broken up into teams.

Training must be scheduled so that it doesn't interfere with peak periods and heavy work schedules. The schedules should be arranged so backup people are available to handle the job responsibilities of the persons being trained.

The single most productive thing a supervisor can do to teach department employees disciplined work habits is to set a good example.

To encourage and motivate employees, recognize and praise accomplishment.

It is often better, and more productive, to retrain a veteran employee whose performance has slipped than it is to find and train someone new for the job.

Classroom training should be organized so the trainer has all relevant material on hand before the training begins.

If the company has an in-house training staff, it's up to the supervisor to communicate to them concerning the skills he wants trainees for the department taught.

Supervisors working for companies without organized training programs can find material and assistance to develop their own programs from a variety of outside sources. These sources include seminars, journals, local education facilities, libraries, trade associations, and retired professionals.

The seating in a classroom depends upon the number of students in the class and the method of teaching.

Homework and night sessions offer dramatic evidence to the students that the training being given is a serious matter. Too much homework, however, may be counterproductive.

Written tests should not be intimidating. They offer some indication as to whether students are paying attention, but they are no guarantee of future job performance.

Expect management to require reports on the effectiveness of all training.

To be effective, training must be planned and it must be complete.

Training never ends. It is a continuous process with something to be learned for everyone, including the supervisor.

6

The Supervisor's "Cheat Sheet," A Short Summary of the Material in This Volume

This chapter is dedicated to those supervisors who are harassed by management, besieged by customers, faced with a dozen deadlines, short of staff, concerned about problems stacking up in the corners like cordwood, and worried about brush fires threatening to become four-alarm blazes. In short, this chapter is dedicated to the typical supervisor at the typical company who has too much to do and not enough time in which to do it.

What some of you may have done is to buy this series in the hope of improving yourself, but now you find it difficult to break away from your duties to go over the material. You're going to get to it someday, sure you are, once those brush fires are out for good. Hey! Isn't that another one blazing away, right there in inventory control?

We have a compromise for you in the form of the following "cheat sheet." It is similar to the ones students use when taking exams. The cheat sheet is a summary of the important information contained in this volume.

Of course you'd be better off reading the entire book. The information in the chapters is more complete and explained in more detail. However, we must be realistic about the many demands on your time. If you're not going to read through the book, whenever you steal a minute or two, skim through this summary. When you find something that applies, or is interesting, go to the specific chapter and look for the bold-type heading on that subject for more complete information.

Even if you have read the entire book, keep this "cheat" chapter close by. It makes a handy reference and memory refresher.

CHAPTER 1, WHY MASTERING COMMUNICATION SKILLS IS IMPORTANT

The supervisor's most important role in the company is that of go-between. Supervisors are like line officers in an army. They take instructions from the top brass and pass them along to the troops. On the reverse side, they obtain information from the troops and pass it along to the high brass. The transfer of information in this manner requires communication skills. *To succeed in your job, learn how to communicate.*

Don't be intimidated by the word. Communications means understanding others and being understood in turn. It sounds simple, but it isn't. What is the best place to start? *The first step in understanding others is learning how to listen.*

The Army teaches plebes at West Point that you have to be able to take directions before you can give them. That applies to supervisors who must take directions from senior management.

Most directions from management can be broken down into three parts:

1. What needs to be done?
2. The means by which it will get done.
3. When it needs to be done.

In any meeting with senior management, listen for these three key issues. *The first rule of communicating with management is to understand what they want done.* Get that part straight and the rest is easy.

What kind of information does management want from the supervisor? That's an easy one too. They want to know what's going on.

Career Hint: *If you want to acquire a reputation as a supervisor who is on top of the job, have a good handle on the status of all projects within your department. Know where you are, know where you are going, and know how you will get there.*

It's important to get things right. At meetings with senior management ask questions and take notes. If something is not clear, say so. State opinions clearly. When speaking, be short and to the point.

After you learn what needs to be done, the message goes to the line employees. When communicating management instructions to the people in your department, plan what you wish to say in advance. The more organized your presentation, the more positive the employees will be about the exercise. Be positive yourself. Use the same care in giving instructions that you took in receiving them. Make sure the employees understand. Give all instructions on a step-by-step basis.

Repetition is an important factor in communication. To get an important point across, say it more than once. Don't be afraid to say the same thing several different ways. (If you read this entire book, you'll find we do that to stress important issues.)

What's the first thing the army does when setting up an outpost? They run a communication line back to headquarters because they need to know what's going on out there. Supervisors need to know what's going on out there too. *The first thing every supervisor should do upon being promoted to the job is to establish an intradepartmental communication system that provides information on everything important that's going on within the department.*

To know what's going on within their department, supervisors must teach their employees how to communicate. Teach communication by:

1. Telling employees why the information is necessary.
2. Being specific on the kind of information that is needed.
3. Making it easy for them to give you needed information.
4. Making sure employees know where and how to get the information.
5. Making sure the information is needed.
6. Reacting quickly when reports aren't turned in on time.
7. Letting employees know how the information is being used.

Supervisors work for organizations and organizations have structure. Sometimes they have requests or demands of employees who work for other departments. When communicating with employees who work in other departments, take that department's supervisor into consideration. You would appreciate a similar courtesy. In fact, learn how to communicate and cooperate with your peers. Working closely with other supervisors can make your job much easier. Supervisors who want cooperation from their peers in other departments must have a clear understanding of and a respect for the other persons' objectives. The key to cooperation is understanding the other person's point of view.

Do you work with customers? Don't regard it as a cross to bear, but rather as a way to be of service. When communicating with customers, remember the rules for communicating with senior management. Listen closely to what they want done. Customers are the most senior management of all. In fact, establish communication skills to communicate with customers, suppliers, and information seekers.

Are you an insider? You need to know what's going on within the company. It's important for all supervisors to be plugged into the company's communication network. Take the time needed to establish yourself as a "terminal" in that network. Cultivate others. Exchange information. It's worth the effort.

CHAPTER 2,
THE COMMUNICATION PROCESS

Ever give a direction and have an employee do exactly the opposite? Does the blame lie with you for not communicating properly or the employee for not understanding? The correct answer is *you*, because management is going to assign you the responsibility no matter who was at fault. That makes it important for supervisors to learn how to communicate precise meanings. Even a small difference between what is meant and what is understood can lead to disaster. Say it simply, say it clearly, say it right, and *make sure the other person understood it the way you said it.*

Good communicators share four common traits. Good communicators are, first, good listeners. They want to hear the other person's message. Listening is a skill that can be acquired through careful practice. To be a good listener you really have to want to learn what the other person has to say.

Good communicators put their own thoughts in order before trying them out on others.

Good communicators speak and write simply and clearly. They recognize that the purpose of communication is to *transfer information.*

Good communicators don't overwhelm the listener with too much information at one time. Instead, they carefully emphasize one or two important points.

Why do some people get the wrong impression even though you have taken pains to be clear? Maybe it's the way you said it. Often, the method of delivery of a message communicates as much as the actual content. Did you maintain a hostile posture? Look angry? Did you say it or write it? Written communications seem more official. A verbal message may seem to be "no big deal."

You give a verbal report to the big boss. What happens next? In most cases the questions begin.

Career Hint: *When reporting information to senior management, always anticipate requests for additional information that is not contained in your report. (They want to get behind the figures to find out what's really going on.) To look "good" in front of the brass, have this information available.*

Think you're helping yourself by running to management with everything that goes wrong? Think again. The truth about problems is that no one really wants to hear about them. (In olden days they killed the messenger who brought bad news.)

Of course there are instances when you have to tell management that trouble's brewing. Just be careful how you do it. Never communicate a problem to management without also suggesting a solution. (It's a fact of corporate life that many problems communicated to management will be ignored.)

Nothing is more embarrassing, or career threatening, to a supervisor than misunderstanding an instruction from senior management and passing along misinformation to line employees. Get instructions right the first time! To make sure they are right, ask questions. Take notes. Learn to take notes you can decipher the next day. When taking notes, don't try to write down everything the speaker says. Concentrate on the major points. Get the *essence* of the remarks.

Management will often give only very general instructions on what needs to be done. It's up to the supervisor to give very specific directions to line employees. (To use a cliche, dot the i's and cross the t's). How to work out the specifics of what needs to be done? When giving detailed instructions to line employees, *work backward from the result desired.* What you want out of a system determines what goes into it. When giving instructions, always ask yourself the following:

1. What is the result I want?

2. What are the steps necessary to achieve this result?

3. How can instructions be simplified so employees know exactly what to do?

4. What additional information or training do my employees need to carry out these instructions?

Are you in the dark about what's going on in the department? To be better informed, learn how to ask the right questions. The first step in framing any question is deciding exactly what you need to know. Ask:

Who?
What?
Where?
When?

Why?

How?

Ask these questions frequently and you'll be well informed.

Do you really understand others? Understanding the people around you is a critical skill for a supervisor. The key to understanding is through paying attention, not only to what is said, but to the person who is saying it. Here are other important points:

> Never assume that the other person has nothing important to say. It's a sure way to miss a lot of important information.

> Never be too busy to listen. Next time the person you ignore may be too busy to tell you something you need to know.

> When meeting with employees give them the courtesy of your full attention. Don't allow interruptions, don't read reports while they're talking, don't take "important" phone calls.

CHAPTER 3,
HOW TO SPEAK SO OTHERS UNDERSTAND YOU

Most communication is verbal. Unfortunately, many verbal requests or directions are misunderstood or misinterpreted by the listener.

The way to reduce misunderstandings (they will never be eliminated) is to be specific and precise when speaking to others.

What you say is important because of your position. More "weight" is attached to anything said by a supervisor simply because the supervisor represents authority to a line employee. That means supervisors must not only think through what they want to say, but how the message will be received.

Manner of speaking is as important as content. A message delivered in a loud voice or angry tone will be received negatively by the listener. The anger will carry far more impact than the actual words used. *The reaction to emotion is almost always emotion.*

Messages also take on significance because of *where* they are delivered. A talk to an employee in the cafeteria will not have the same impact as the same words said in the supervisor's office.

Directions and instructions must be delivered firmly. The employee must never be left with any doubt about the need to carry them out.

When giving instructions always ask for verbal feedback. You'll be shocked to learn how many times a simple message gets twisted. Feedback allows the opportunity for corrections.

When giving orders to employees, also provide an explanation as to why they are necessary. They deserve that courtesy. Allow questions. Listen to suggestions. If someone offers a suggestion on how to do the job better, by all means take it. Give seasoned employees credit for knowing their jobs.

Display a positive attitude when giving directions. *Never be apologetic.* Never blame senior management for making changes. Trying to improve things is their job.

Anticipate objections whenever giving directions. *Anticipate many, many objections when the directions involve something new.*

Do your people complain a lot? Are the complaints a chorus when something new is required? That's the supervisor's fate. It's up to the supervisor to separate complaints from legitimate concerns.

Want to take the sting out of employee's concern over a

new system? Want to inject a little morale in the team? To instill team spirit and build morale, *do some of the dirty work yourself.* Nothing improves employees' attitude about a project more than seeing the boss pitch in and help.

What's the difference between verbal and written message? It's in their life spans. A written message can become a permanent part of the company archives. It's ageless, around forever, perhaps to haunt the person who wrote it. On the other hand, once a verbal message has been delivered, it is lost in the ozone. It is difficult to reconstruct exactly what was said, the tone that was used, or even the statement that was actually made.

Many of us have poor speaking habits. What are these habits?

1. We don't think through what we want to say.

2. We don't choose words carefully.

3. We don't consider the listener's reaction.

4. We don't pick the proper time and place.

5. We don't speak clearly.

6. We aren't really interested in our own messages *and the lack of commitment shows through.*

A briefing is a meeting at which a detailed plan of action is revealed to employees. *The success of any plan always depends on how well the details are communicated.* Want a plan to succeed? Take the time to make sure that employees know what is to be done. (Running any successful business meeting requires advance preparation and planning.)

Meetings and briefings go more smoothly when trusted subordinates are involved in working out the details of the program. (Which means, of course, that you're going to have to learn to trust your subordinates.)

Here are eight tips for making a business meeting a success.

1. Have a good reason for calling the meeting. This seems obvious, but far too many meetings have obscure agendas.
2. Set a timetable and keep to it.
3. Invite only those parties with a keen interest in the subject.
4. Give all attendees advance notice of what will be discussed.
5. Make sure the meeting room is prepared and contains everything needed.
6. Make the presentations lively.
7. Encourage audience participation.
8. Provide a written summary.

Management often judges the abilities of supervisors based on the impressions they make when giving presentations. Supervisors should look upon such presentations as career opportunities and prepare accordingly. *Whenever you're talking to senior management, you're on stage.*

Never hide bad news when meeting with senior management. The sooner bad news is out in the open, the less negative impact it will have on a supervisor's reputation.

Every manager, every supervisor, at every level in every corporation must be "selling" something at least some of the time. Get used to it. The entire fabric of corporate life is based on evaluating one proposition after another. Management picks and chooses from a wide variety of options. Learn how to sell your ideas. What sells an idea? Management is persuaded by *enthusiasm and commitment.* Stand behind your propositions.

Supervisors are regarded by management and line employees alike as the "hands-on" people with the answers.

Answers to what? Just about everything under the sun. Those supervisors who learn how to handle questions make their jobs much easier. If there is one key to answering questions, it is to *anticipate the questions that will be asked.* Know what will be asked and, of course, know the answer.

It is a fact of corporate life that supervisors will receive objections whenever changes are made or employees are asked to do something new. Employees will have all kinds of reasons why they can't possibly do what they have been asked to do. It's up to the supervisor to sort out the legitimate concerns from those that are based on resistance to change. Also remember that *it is not necessary to answer every objection.* If there are ten good things that will result from something being done, they will outweigh one small negative result.

It would be dandy if supervisors could do their work without interruptions, but that will never happen. Too many things are going on in most work environments. There are questions, problems, emergencies, phone calls, staff meetings, and so forth. All these deflect from the supervisor's mission, which is to get the work out. The way to handle interruptions and still maintain a normal work load is as follows:

1. Come into the office or plant early.
2. Don't allow the telephone to become a tyrant. The world won't end if you don't respond immediately to every phone call.
3. Delegate responsibilities. (If you give people authority to make decisions, they won't have to come to you for everything.)
4. Be neat and organized. This strategy will help you remember where you were if interrupted,

Ever since Marc Anthony gave a funeral oration for Julius Caesar, public speaking has made many people nervous. What are they afraid of? Making fools of themselves.

Who wants to look like an idiot? Familiarity is the antidote for fear. The best way to stop being afraid of speaking in public is to practice. Speak before groups whenever you can. Make a pest of yourself before your spouse and your children. Practicing won't eliminate the fears, but it will reduce them.

There is something that works even better than practicing. That is to *have something worthwhile to say*. The first rule of speechmaking is to make the talk interesting. If the audience members are fascinated by the material, they won't notice little hesitations and stumbles by the speaker.

Here are some other ideas when speaking before a group:

Use a style that is natural for you.

Establish eye contact with someone in the audience.

Employ language that people in the audience will understand.

Be brief and to the point.

Present the material in a logical sequence.

Don't give the impression of being pompous and self-important.

Take your time. The audience will wait for you.

Engage the emotions of the audience. They will remember passion and enthusiasm.

Establish a rapport with the audience.

Tailor your speech to fit the audience.

Ask yourself, "What do you know that the audience wants to know?" Compose your speech accordingly.

Use cue cards and other memory joggers.

Give hand-outs that cover the content of your remarks.

Repeat the important points several times.

Put a few surprises in your speech. The audience will remember what surprises them.

Be sure the audience is getting the message. Watch the audience. Do they look interested? Is anyone walking out prematurely? Does the audience seem responsive? Is there a collective sigh of relief when you finish? The way to get feedback from a speech is by asking for it. Solicit comments. Also pass out question cards. Ask questions. Get people involved.

CHAPTER 4,
HOW TO WRITE SO OTHERS UNDERSTAND

Many supervisors with good oral communication skills are intimidated when it's time to put things in writing. Writing it all down seems so much more final. However, writing reports, making written observations and suggestions, communicating information to management, providing written directives, and so forth is an important part of most supervisors' jobs. It's a skill they must somehow acquire.

The first thing to do when staring at a blank sheet of paper is to think about your purpose. Focus on what you wish to communicate. Using an outline before beginning any writing can make the task easier. Outlines help organize material and help the writer determine what's really important. It also helps the writer make sure all important points were covered.

Ask yourself who, exactly, will read what you've written? The question is important because the audience determines both what you write and how you write it. After defining the audience, the big question to ask yourself is, "What do I want them to learn from this communication?"

Good writing connects the reader to the writer. The way to write "good" is to use simple declarative sentences. Don't package too many ideas in a single correspondence. When finished writing, read through your own material to make sure you understand it. If you have difficulty figuring out what you meant, you can be sure the reader will too. If the writing seems confusing, *tear it up and begin again.* All writers rewrite. They hone and polish their material.

When writing, help yourself by acquiring the following "assistance":

> Legal-size notepads
>
> A word processor
>
> A good dictionary and thesaurus
>
> A book on grammar and style

Most of what a supervisor writes will come in the form of memos. Memos are internal, informal, written communications. They should be short, clear, and accurate. There's nothing wrong with a one-sentence memo. (Just as a boxer does, get in, land your punch, and get out.)

Supervisors often use the memo form to issue instructions to line employees. The typical elements in an instruction type memo are

> What is to be done
>
> Why it is to be done
>
> How it is to be done
>
> When it is to be done

Include these parts and *make yourself clear*, and you've written the perfect instruction memo.

Memos to senior management usually contain information or make requests. Others are written "for the record" (to shield the writer from blame). If your memos are being ignored, perhaps you are writing too many of them. Aside from scheduled reports, senior management wants to hear from you only when things go wrong. When you do bring up a problem, you had better have an idea in mind on a fix.

A written report is an information transfer.

In any company a supervisor's reputation rides on two things:

1. How well his or her department is performing
2. The clarity of his or her written reports

Do a good job, but write murky reports, and you won't be as well regarded as the supervisor who is able to communicate, even though the latter's departmental performance may be mediocre.

What management wants in a report is accurate information provided in a format that is easy to read and simple to understand. The shorter the report, the better.

A business proposal is a written argument trying to persuade management to do something. Its goal is to get management excited enough to act. Proposals present a problem, offer a solution to that problem, and detail the benefits of that solution. Whenever presenting a proposal to management, be prepared to give it both orally and in written form. Make sure the proposal contains no surprises by meeting with management in advance to go over the essence of your proposition.

Get ideas accepted by making them come alive. Use graphs, charts, and other visual displays whenever possible to dramatize ideas. A graph or a chart makes numerical comparisons much clearer.

It's not enough for supervisors to acquire communication skills; they must train their staff members to acquire them as well. To monitor the department's work flow, supervisors depend on a steady stream of information from line employees. That makes it important for the supervisor to teach their employees simple written communication skills. This can be done by

1. Making sure all employees know what kind of information is needed.
2. Making reporting as simple as possible.
3. Encouraging classes to improve writing skills.

4. Writing simply yourself to encourage the style.

Supervisors are required to correspond with customers for many different reasons. An important rule of business correspondence is *the shorter the letter, the more likely it will achieve the desired result.*

When writing business letters, get to the reason for the correspondence in the first sentence. Don't wander, but stick to the purpose. Say what must be said and *finish*!

CHAPTER 5, HOW TO TRAIN EMPLOYEES

In many companies, training consists of a raw recruit being shown the ropes for a day or two by a seasoned employee and then left on his own to sink or swim. This system inevitably leaves gaps in the trainee's knowledge and "fill-in" sessions to teach what should have been taught initially. Inadequately trained personnel can hurt the performance of the department.

It is the supervisor's first responsibility to "sell" the company on the value of a good training program. Training is key to a supervisor's personal success. The well-trained crew that functions smoothly and delivers results month after month makes the supervisor look good.

The learning process is never finished, which means training must be continuous. Retraining is also important because people forget what they know.

The first step in a training program is to develop a set of objectives. The first objective is obvious:

The goal of all business training is to produce competent, self-sufficient employees who can function without constant supervision.

Testing new employees and retesting veterans is important to assess training needs. *You need to find out what employees already know.*

Students coming out of our current education system may lack basic skills needed to perform must jobs. It's up to business, which means it's up to the supervisor, to provide these skills. *Don't assume any level of knowledge or skill on the part of new employees. Find out!*

On-the-job training is the most popular training format. However, unless the training is planned and organized, this form of training can lead to information gaps in the person being trained. Begin an on-the-job training program by making a list of everything the trainee needs to know to perform.

Classroom training works best when there are a number of people to be trained. It is also appropriate when introducing new equipment or a new system.

There are two styles of classroom training: lecture and workshop.

Lecturing can become boring for the students unless it is broken up with demonstrations, guest speakers, hands-on sessions, and so forth.

In workshop training students are broken up into teams and given problems to solve. This kind of training provides a competitive atmosphere in which teams strive for better solutions. The students learn from the exercise, from other team members, and from rival teams.

Before beginning classroom training the trainer should make certain that all material needed during the sessions is available.

Any class becomes more lively when students participate via discussions, student presentations, question-and-answer sessions, practice demonstrations, and so forth.

How the classroom is set up depends on the number of

students in the class, the type of training, and the degree of control the instructor wishes to maintain.

Night sessions and homework are dramatic symbols that the training is a serious matter. However, students shouldn't be so forced to burn the midnight oil to complete homework assignments that they are unable to pay adequate attention during class.

Written tests have value because they show who has been listening and "getting" the material, but they do not offer proof of who will actually do better on the job. *Tests don't represent the real workplace.*

To keep the department running efficiently, veteran employees should be retrained on a regular basis. There is no such person as an employee who is completely trained. Retraining veterans, however, sometimes bruises fragile egos. Introduce the training in such a manner so the veteran is not offended.

In the practical world, training must be scheduled so that it doesn't interfere or interrupt work flow.

Want to teach your employees good habits? *Set a good example.* Nothing is more important. The supervisor sets the pace for the entire department. Classroom and/or on-the-job training is never enough to produce dedicated employees. The missing ingredient is attitude which is instilled by the supervisor providing the right kind of example.

Supervisors who have the benefit of an in-house professional training staff should make use of them. It is up to the supervisor to communicate with professional trainers concerning their training needs. Tell them about the requirements of your department.

Supervisors who are required to develop their own training programs can get help from seminars, journals and bulletins, local educational facilities, local libraries, retired professionals, and trade associations.

When training is completed, expect management to require a report on the results. When writing such a report, keep it simple, cover all the bases, and give an honest appraisal.

I N D E X